do-it-yourself do-it-yourself
do-it-yourself do-it-yourself
do-it-yourself do-it-yourself
do-it-yourself do-it-yourself
do-it-yourself do-it-yourself
do-it-yourself do-it-yourself
do-it-yourself do-it-yourself
do-it-yourself do-it-yourself
do-it-yourself do-it-yourself
do-it-yourself do-it-yourself
do-it-yourself do-it-yourself
do-it-yourself do-it-yourself
do-it-yourself do-it-yourself
do-it-yourself do-it-yourself
do-it-yourself do-it-yourself
do-it-yourself do-it-yourself
do-it-yourself do-it-yourself
do-it-yourself do-it-yourself
do-it-yourself do-it-yourself
do-it-yourself do-it-yourself
do-it-yourself do-it-yourself
do-it-yourself do-it-yourself
do-it-yourself do-it-yourself
do-it-yourself do-it-yourself
do-it-yourself do-it-yourself
do-it-yourself do-it-yourself
do-it-yourself do-it-yourself
do-it-yourself do-it-yourself
do-it-yourself do-it-yourself
do-it-yourself do-it-yourself
do-it-yourself do-it-yourself
do-it-yourself do-it-yourself
do-it-yourself do-it-yourself
do-it-yourself do-it-yourself
do-it-yourself do-it-yourself
do-it-yourself do-it-yourself
do-it-yourself do-it-yourself
do-it-yourself do-it-yourself
do-it-yourself do-it-yourself
do-it-yourself do-it-yourself
do-it-yourself do-it-yourself
do-it-yourself do-it-yourself
do-it-yourself do-it-yourself
do-it-yourself do-it-yourself
do-it-yourself do-it-yourself

INTERIOR
HOME REPAIRS

do-it-yourself do-it-yourself
do-it-yourself do-it-yourself
do-it-yourself do-it-yourself
do-it-yourself do-it-yourself
do-it-yourself do-it-yourself
do-it-yourself do-it-yourself
do-it-yourself do-it-yourself
do-it-yourself do-it-yourself
do-it-yourself do-it-yourself
do-it-yourself do-it-yourself
do-it-yourself do-it-yourself
do-it-yourself do-it-yourself
do-it-yourself do-it-yourself
do-it-yourself do-it-yourself
do-it-yourself do-it-yourself
do-it-yourself do-it-yourself
do-it-yourself do-it-yourself
do-it-yourself do-it-yourself
do-it-yourself do-it-yourself
do-it-yourself do-it-yourself
do-it-yourself do-it-yourself
do-it-yourself do-it-yourself
do-it-yourself do-it-yourself
do-it-yourself do-it-yourself
do-it-yourself do-it-yourself
do-it-yourself do-it-yourself
do-it-yourself do-it-yourself
do-it-yourself do-it-yourself
do-it-yourself do-it-yourself
do-it-yourself do-it-yourself
do-it-yourself do-it-yourself
do-it-yourself do-it-yourself
do-it-yourself do-it-yourself
do-it-yourself do-it-yourself
do-it-yourself do-it-yourself
do-it-yourself do-it-yourself

Editor-in Chief and Series Coordinator
DONALD D. WOLF
Design, Layout and Production
MARGOT L. WOLF

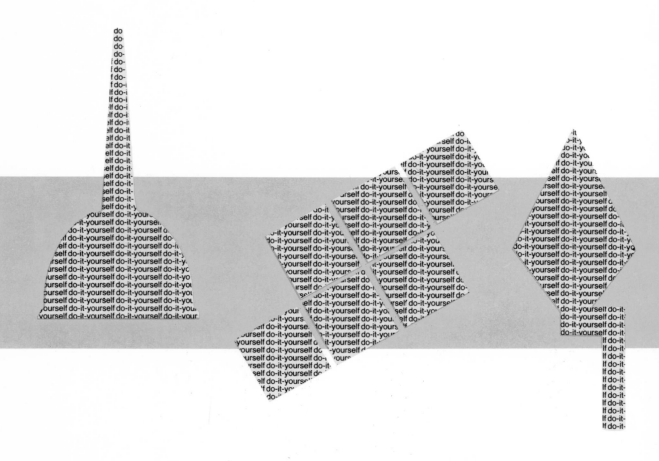

ADVENTURES IN HOME REPAIR SERIES

INTERIOR HOME REPAIRS

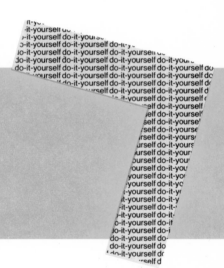

Written by
DICK DEMSKE
Illustrated by
JAMES E. BARRY

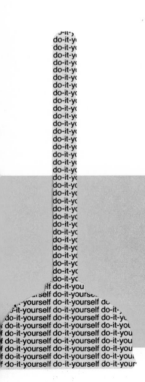

Consolidated Book Publishers

NEW YORK • CHICAGO

Introduction

Welcome to the club.

It is not exactly an exclusive club. Its membership includes virtually everyone who owns a home or lives in an apartment in this country and probably in the world. All you need do to join is pick up a hammer or screwdriver or bathroom plunger and perform one of the small but essential maintenance tasks associated with modern living—repair a squeaking floor, free a stuck window, open a clogged drain. For, unless you have a full staff of servants to deal with such mundane matters, you will probably end up doing at least most of them yourself, for reasons economic, expedient, and essential.

So, welcome to the club. We would like to think of this book as a sort of club member's manual, because it tells you what you need to know to deal with the most common problems you are likely to encounter and, in so doing, make your encounters that much more tolerable—if not pleasurable, at least tolerable. After all, nobody likes it when things go wrong, but setting things right again has its own obvious rewards.

Not everyone will be able to perform all the chores described herein himself or herself. Most of the home maintenance and repair procedures are relatively simple; if you wish to undertake more extensive repairs or remodeling projects, we suggest that you consult other books in this series, such as *Plumbing* and *Electricity*. To help you determine whether a specific job falls within your range of capabilities, we have consulted with professional carpenters, plumbers, electricians, and home-repair contractors, and with manufacturers of various home products, to rate the degree of difficulty of each operation. Those marked ● should pose no problems for the average person with reasonable dexterity. Those with an ▲ rating require a bit more skill and experience but are still well within the do-it-yourselfer's domain. Projects marked ■ are on the difficult side and should be left to the professionals unless you have advanced skills and knowledge.

Every effort has been made to ensure the accuracy, reliability, and up-to-dateness of the information and instructions in this book. We are not infallible, however—and neither are you. We cannot guarantee that there are no human or typographical errors herein, nor can we guarantee that you will not err in following our directions. We only hope that, if this happens, it will not lessen the feeling of satisfaction you receive from doing-it-yourself.

DONALD D. WOLF

Contents

1

Do-It-Yourself Home Repairs

Your home represents a very large and very important investment, and one that should be treated wisely and well. Both old and new houses, no matter how carefully they are built, need occasional repairs to keep them in good condition and to retard depreciation. Like anything else, a house deteriorates and declines in value if it is not properly cared for.

WHAT TO LOOK FOR

Careful attention to signs of wear can often eliminate the need for major repairs that stem from neglected minor problems. A sticking window can cause breakage of glass; faulty plumbing can cause damage to a plaster ceiling; a defective electrical fixture can cause a disastrous fire. These and similar difficulties can be avoided by proper and frequent inspections and prompt correction of the usually trivial sources of trouble. It's simply a matter of a stitch in time.

Who should make that stitch? Repairs that require specialized knowledge and skills should be performed only by qualified persons. But most repairs can be undertaken by any homeowner or apartment dweller who is handy with tools. In fact, with the virtual disappearance of the "neighborhood handyman" and the increasing reluctance of apartment "supers" to perform many minor maintenance chores, the do-it-

yourselfer is often the only one who can halt the little irritations before they develop into big—and expensive—headaches.

Of course, economics enters into it as well. The money you save by doing your own maintenance and small repairs can be

Sticking window may lead to broken glass.

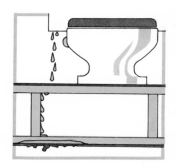

Faulty plumbing can cause damaged ceiling.

Faulty electrical fixture is dangerous.

wisely invested in home improvements to enhance the value of your house and make living in it more enjoyable and more comfortable. But this is not your only motivation, nor may it even be the major one. Pride of ownership compels a person to work hard to maintain and improve the home. This pride is considerably heightened when combined with the joy of personal accomplishment. Often a home handyperson may feel, somewhat vainly but understandably, that no one else can do the job quite the way he or she wants it done, or quite as well as he/she might do it. This may not be false reasoning, either, for certainly the tender, loving care that a do-it-yourselfer puts into a project must count for something. Add to the joy of accomplishment the pleasure that many people experience when working with their hands. It's a fine form of relaxation, with the very practical reward of contributing something to keeping your home more comfortable, safe, and enjoyable.

Of course, not all do-it-yourselfers can do all the many chores required to keep a home in tiptop shape. Some people, whose hands may seem composed totally of thumbs, should shy away from even picking up a hammer lest they bring down the house about themselves. For them, we can only hope that they are lucky enough to find that vanishing species of neighborhood handyman. Others live in dread fear of drowning if a toilet overflows, or of electrocution every time they switch on a lamp. To them, we suggest that they post the numbers of a competent plumber and electrician next to the telephone and ring them up at the first hint of trouble.

But for the vast majority of homeowners and apartment dwellers, a regular program of inspection and maintenance will be simple and rewarding. You may be pleasantly surprised to learn how much you *can* do.

2

Before You Buy a House

WHAT FIRST APPEARS to be a bargain home may turn out to be a headache. A thorough inspection may reveal hidden defects and obvious remodeling needs.

Few people make a full-time business of checking house construction. If you have doubts about the soundness of the house you have selected, obtain an expert appraisal of the property to establish its value and point out deficiencies. In many cities there are reputable inspection firms that will examine the home and give you a detailed report. The $50 or $100 fee may be well spent. Some buyers face the expense of replacing basic equipment within the first year of ownership. If you have doubts about the wiring, plumbing, or heating plant, the owner may permit you to have it checked by an expert. You must be prepared to pay for this inspection. If the plumbing system includes a septic tank, an expert should definitely check the equipment before you purchase.

If you must call in experts, first check their reputations and beware of unscrupulous operators who may justify their fee by exaggerating flaws, which they may want to repair at inflated costs.

The age of a house should not necessarily limit your choice. Although older homes may require more repair work, many have received excellent care from previous longtime owners and compare favorably with newer structures. If it appears that repairs and improvements are needed, be sure to secure advance estimates of the cost of the work and find out who will pay for it—you or the seller.

A home inspection should be conducted in a systematic manner, beginning with the basement. Most of the common problems encountered can be fixed by the average do-it-yourselfer. Some require calling in a pro. Really major defects may lead you to decide against buying—why buy trouble?

FOUNDATION DEFECTS

If the foundation walls are solid concrete, they should be examined for cracks; if they are of unit masonry, the joints should be examined to see that no mortar is loose or has fallen out. The basement floor should be examined for cracks or signs of disintegration, and any evidence of leakage through the walls or floor should be noted.

Check joints on concrete block wall that no mortar is loose.

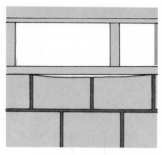

Make sure sill joints are tight and do not admit light, air, or moisture.

Check joists, bridging for sagging.

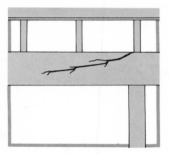

Inspect beams for cracks or shrinkage.

Check floors for level.

Inspect basement steps.

Check basement framing for signs of termites, rot.

Wooden stills on top of the foundation walls should be examined to see that they are sound and that there are no uncalked cracks between wall and sills to admit moisture and cold air.

If the basement has no ceiling, the joists should be examined for signs of sagging or warping. These defects often occur because the support or bridging is not adequate. Look for excessive shrinkage in the floor framing.

Girders and beams that support the first-floor joists should be examined for settlement, sagging, and, if the material is wood, shrinkage. A carpenter's level placed on the finish flooring of the first floor, both across and along the direction of the floor joists near points of support, should indicate whether column or wall footings have settled or whether there has been shrinkage in girders. Settlement, sagging, or shrinkage of floor supports may distort the shape of door frames in partitions and prevent proper closing of the doors.

Treads and stringers of basement steps should be examined to determine that they are sound and securely fastened. Basement steps should have at least one handrail that is solidly fastened. The steps should be well lighted along their entire length.

Check for signs of damage caused by termites or other destructive insects in posts, sills, joists, and other woodwork. Look also for evidence of decay from dry rot, especially in sills and at ends of joists adjoining masonry.

Make sure that all exposed water pipes are protected from freezing, especially if located under a porch or in some other unheated space. If there are floor drains in the basement or garage, see that there is sufficient water in them to maintain a seal in the traps.

HEATING EQUIPMENT

■Because there are many types of heating systems, the details of inspection necessarily vary. The most favorable time for this inspection is in the spring when the plant is shut down for the season. If you have the heating plant inspected, try to find someone who is not also a salesman for a furnace company.

Check all radiator valves and shut-off cocks for possible leakage, and, in the case of a hot-water heating system, see that the boiler and radiators contain sufficient water. This is an indication of how well the owner has maintained the equipment. Examine the furnace or boiler to see whether grates or burners need repair or adjustment. See if there are cracks in the boiler and whether the firebox and clean-out doors fit tightly. Examine the condition of insulation on boiler, hot-water tank, pipes, and ducts to see whether new or additional covering is needed. Filters, humidifier fans,

grills, and registers used with warm-air systems should also be inspected for possible defects.

Examine the chimney to see if the mortar needs pointing and whether the cement is sound around the smoke pipe where it enters the chimney. Notice whether woodwork adjoining the chimney requires fireproof covering to lessen fire hazard.

DOORS, WINDOWS, FLOORS, WALLS

Defects in the interior of a house are generally more apparent than those on the outside. A clogged drain, a leaky faucet, a sticking door or window usually attract attention, but other faults may go unnoticed unless carefully inspected. Examine all doors to see how true they hang and to find out if they stick. The lock or latch should be examined to see that the strike plate is not so far out of line that the door cannot easily be locked or latched. Raise and lower all windows to learn how they slide and whether cords or other parts need replacement. Observe how the sash fits, and see if weatherstripping is needed around the windows or doors. Notice whether there are any openings in or around the screens where insects can enter. All these little things can add up to a lot of aggravation after you have moved into the house.

If baseboards do not fit snugly to the floor, it is usually because they have

Inspect chimney for loose mortar, smoke pipe for corrosion.

Check radiators for possible leakage.

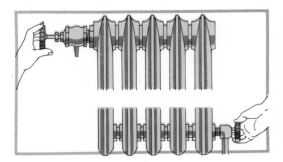

Make sure that screens fit snugly.

shrunk, but in some cases the settling of floor supports causes this condition. Creaking in a floor may be detected by bearing heavily upon various sections of it. Flooring should be examined for wear and looseness, stair treads for loose or defective coverings, and handrails for stability.

Look for cracks in the drywall or plaster, particularly over door openings, and see

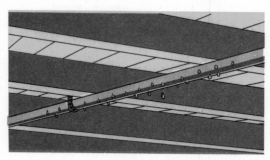

Pipes in exposed areas have to be properly insulated.

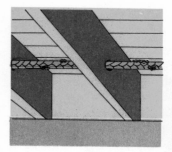

Examine exposed wiring for conditon of insulation.

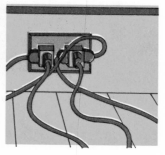

Beware of extension cords.

whether the plaster on the ceiling is cracked or loose. Other types of interior finishes such as paneling should be examined for buckling, loosening, cracking, or breakage.

HOUSEHOLD EQUIPMENT

When the structure of the house has been inspected, it is advisable to examine all equipment in which trouble could develop.

Plumbing facilities, including water-supply and drainage piping, fixtures, and equipment, should be checked to see that all parts of the system are in good condition and functioning properly. Drains and traps should be inspected for possible clogging, faucets for leaks, and flush valves or mechanisms in toilet flush tanks to see whether repairs or new parts are needed. Determine whether exposed piping is properly insulated against freezing in winter or moisture condensation during the summer. Examine all exposed wiring to see that the insulation is in good condition. If electrical appliances are included with the house, inspect the cords to see if they are in good condition. Check the operation of all appliances.

As a matter of expediency, the homeowner may frequently use an extension cord to supply an area not provided with a convenience outlet. Although this is satisfactory for temporary use, it should not continue as a substitute for a permanent outlet. Make sure there are plenty of electrical outlets.

3

Routine Maintenance

Do-IT-YOURSELF home care knows no seasons. Most homeowners make a year-round project of keeping their places in tiptop shape—after all, it's a matter of pride of possession. But some jobs are seasonal, or at least are better done at one time than another. Intended only as a general guide, this seasonal checklist will help you schedule regular maintenance around the house. Of course, much of the actual scheduling depends on the climate of the area in which you live, but the list will help to remind you when it's time to do what.

SEASONAL CHECKLIST

January

- Give yourself a few days to let the shock of the holidays wear off, then make a New Year's resolution to keep things in top shape for the next twelve months. You can start by repairing all those annoying squeaks and squeals in the floors and stairs that betrayed you every time you came tiptoeing in late at night after one of those many holiday office parties.
- And it's a good time to check out the plumbing, especially those leaky faucets that have advanced from drip-drips to roaring deluges. Some washers should do the trick. Drains that go glug-glug and pipes that go bang-bang should also be silenced, as well as the toilet tank that doesn't know enough to shut up (or off).
- As long as you are on a quiet kick, pick up a kit of household oil, stick lubricants, and the like and take a quick trip about the house, treating hinges, appliance doors, chairs, furniture casters, drawers, and whatever else might squeak (or stick). By now you ought to have the quietest and slickest house in the neighborhood.
- But don't let all that quiet put you to sleep—there is one more job to do. Make it a regular practice to open the faucet at the bottom of the hot-water heater and drain off any rusty water. This will help to insure long life for that hard-working appliance.

February

- Winter weather starting to get on your nerves? Perk up with a touch-up campaign, repairing and refinishing chips and nicks in furniture, cabinets, and porcelain fixtures.
- It's a good time, too, to patch any plaster cracks that have made their appearance during the cold months.
- With winter waning, this might be the

time to refinish hardwood floors that are showing signs of heavy wear worsened by wet-weather traffic.

March

● Whether the month comes in like a lion or a lamb, you know that spring can't be too far off. How about repairing and repainting the outdoor furniture so that it will be ready when those nice days finally arrive.

● Before you know it, screen time will be here. Now is your chance to make any necessary repairs—before the bugs come around.

● When the spring thaw comes, make a close check for leaks, particularly around doors and windows. Remember that April showers are on the way, and be prepared.

April

▲ Those April showers will bring May flowers—and a lush new growth of lawn. Get that lawnmower in shape, making needed mechanical repairs, sharpening the blade, and lubricating according to the manufacturer's instructions.

● Once again it's time to drain off any rusty water that has accumulated in the hot-water heater.

May

▲ Air conditioner in shape? You'll be needing it any day now, so make needed repairs and follow the manufacturer's directions for preseason maintenance (check owner's manual).

● While you are in an electrical frame of mind, how about repairing lamps, small appliances, nonworking fixtures, and faulty switches that have accumulated over the winter.

June

● Bug time, but don't let them bug you. The first line of defense is screening to keep them out, so make sure that a screen is repaired immediately after your neighbor's daughter blasts a home-run ball through it. Also make sure that you have the proper pesticides on hand to fight off those little beasties that make it through the outer defense line (see CHAPTER 11).

● Summer water shortages are becoming increasingly common in many areas, so guard against water wastage by making sure that dripping faucets and running toilets are promptly repaired.

July

● Muggy weather can cause excessive condensation inside the house, which in turn can cause drawers, doors, and windows to stick and, in extreme cases, damage to floors, walls, and ceilings. Take corrective action as necessary.

● Don't let the hot weather make you forget that it's time to drain off the water heater again.

August

● If you have been a diligent weekend handyman all year long, you have earned a vacation this month, so head for the mountains or the shore, or just relax in your backyard with a cool drink and ponder the pitiful plight of your neighbor who has put off all his home-care projects until now.

September

● Old Man Winter may still seem to be far off, especially on those "dog days," but he is heading your way, so get ready for him. Make sure your house is weathertight, calking around doors and windows where necessary and installing weatherstripping if it is needed. Repair any damaged storm sash.

▲ Don't wait for a cold snap to get your heating system in shape. Have it cleaned (or do it yourself, but this can be a messy job). Replace filters, check boilers and humidifiers, etc. Make sure the smoke pipe between furnace and chimney is solid and not leaking or corroded. If in doubt, replace it.

October

- Don't let the World Series distract you—now you *have* to get ready for winter. Between innings, check your basement walls for cracks that could cause trouble under cold-weather pressures. At halftime of the College Game-of-the-Week, make a prewinter calk walk around the house, filling cracks and joints between various components and dissimilar materials. It will give you peace of mind come Super Bowl time.
- Time, too, to retire outdoor furniture and accessories; make sure they are properly protected during the nasty months—especially if you store them in a damp or exposed area.
- It's time again to—guess what? That's it, drain the hot-water heater. It's paying attention to regular tasks like this that means long, trouble-free life for your home and its equipment.

November

- With the chill winds starting to blow, make sure that weatherstripping around doors and windows is snugly in place.
- Turn off the water supply to outside faucets and drain these lines to avoid freezing problems.

- Holiday season is on the way, so this is a good time to fix up and paint up. Repair plaster cracks and rejuvenate rooms with a new coat of paint or a bright modern wallpaper print. This might also be the time to put down that new vinyl floor in the kitchen, or to tile the bathroom walls.

December

- It's a good idea to be prepared for wintertime emergencies, so get together a kit and be ready for the worst, while hoping for the best. Include such items as plastic sheet (in case a storm breaks a window or pokes a hole in the roof), staple gun, shovel, hammer and nails, lanterns or flashlights, calking gun, etc.
- Before you put that string of lights on the Christmas tree, check carefully to make sure that the wires are in good condition—not frayed or exposed at the sockets. And while you are at it, check out lamp and appliance cords throughout the house and make any necessary repairs, as described in CHAPTER 13.
- You've done a good year's work, so now you deserve to relax with a cup of eggnog before starting the New Year. Cheers!

The wintertime emergency arsenal.

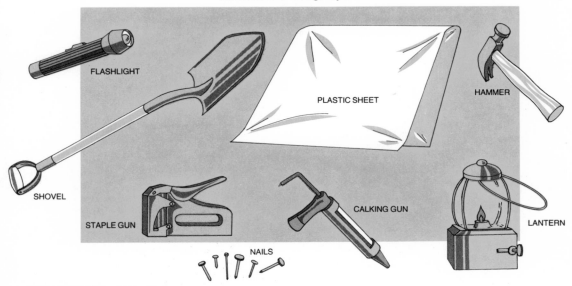

FLASHLIGHT

PLASTIC SHEET

HAMMER

SHOVEL

STAPLE GUN

CALKING GUN

LANTERN

NAILS

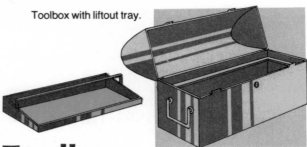

Toolbox with liftout tray.

4

The Basic Toolbox

ALL THE HOW-TO talent in the world won't help you if you don't have a proper set of tools. Don't make the mistake of going out and investing a small or large fortune in whatever the local hardware store has in stock, but—if you are new to the interior-repairs game—have on hand a few basic items. You can buy others as the need arises.

Never bargain-shop for tools. Don't settle for a lesser type or smaller size than you really need. And don't skimp on quality. A penny saved can mean dollars lost—or worse. Whatever the tool, look for a sturdy body and smooth finish. Metal surfaces should be coated for rust prevention; wood parts should be varnished, waxed, or lacquered for durability and protection against splinters.

Check all moving parts of a tool before purchase to make sure that they work smoothly and easily but are free of any play or wiggle. Look for tools that are permanently marked with the manufacturer's name or symbol as an indication of careful construction and quality materials. Some quality tools even have performance warranties.

For keeping your tools in good condition, a simple toolbox can be a prudent investment. It will help protect them from dust and moisture and provide a convenient organizer, storage space, and carrying case as well.

Certain basic safety tips apply to tool usage, regardless of what the tool may be:

- Never use a tool with a dulled cutting blade or bit or a loose part.
- Use tools only for the work they were intended to do. Never use a screwdriver to pry, chip, or pound; a wood bit to drill masonry or metal; pliers to pound or cut taut wire, or a wrench to hammer.
- Never expose pliers, screwdrivers, or wrenches to extreme heat; they could become weakened and suddenly give way during use.
- Do not try to repair a tool yourself unless you know what you are doing. Either buy a new one or take the crippled tool to an expert.

NAIL HAMMER

You need no introduction to the nail hammer—the tool for driving common or finishing nails, tacks, or staples into wood, plaster, or wallboard and for extracting nails. But you do need to consider certain important features when you buy one.

A slightly domed striking face allows you to drive nails flush without marring the surrounding surface. Curved claws, with inside edges beveled sharp, slip under a nail head to grip the shank for smooth removal. A hammer head set at a slightly acute angle to the handle helps you hit squarely. A handle may be steel or fiberglass with a rubber or plastic grip, or it may be wood. A wood handle should be firmly wedged or glued into the head.

The 16-ounce nail hammer is suitable for most uses and can be purchased for about $5 at any hardware store.

SCREWDRIVER

Another familiar tool is the screwdriver, designed to provide good turning leverage for driving and removing screws. It comes in two basic styles. The flat-tip style is for the single slot screws used in walls, woodwork, and furniture. The Phillips fits the cross-slotted screws found on many home appliances. If you don't own at least one of each, you should buy them, keeping the following points in mind.

The most generally useful flat-tip model has a wedge-shaped end about ¼ inch wide and a blade about 6 inches long. It costs about a dollar. A No. 2 Phillips with a 4-inch blade works on most cross-slotted screws and also costs about a dollar. Either style should have a large, fluted handle with a gently rounded butt end for firm, comfortable gripping. If compact storage is desirable, look for a model with a detachable, reversible blade—flat-tipped at one end and Phillips style at the other.

Assorted tip sizes and blade lengths may be a good investment if you use tools often. A flat-tip driver wider than the screw will scar the surrounding surface; a tip too narrow gives poor leverage and may damage the screw slot. Shorter blades are helpful in cramped quarters. Either prepackaged sets or three flat-tipped drivers—4, 6, and 8 inches—plus a No. 1 and No. 2 Phillips meet most household needs.

HAND DRILL

To insert long screws or bolts into or through wood, plaster, or wallboard, you first need to make neat, straight holes for

Nail hammer.

Phillips screwdriver (above).

Too-wide scrwdriver
(above right).

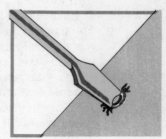

Flat-tip screwdriver.

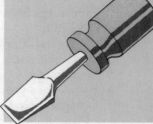

Stubby screwdriver (right).

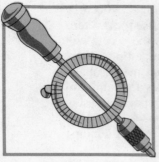

Rotary-crank drill.

Push drill.

Slip-joint pliers.

Adjustable wrench.

them. Either a rotary cranking or a push-style hand drill can do the job. Each is sold with interchangeable bits for making holes at least ¾ inch deep and up to ¼ inch wide. The handles are hollow for bit storage, and replacement bits are available at most hardware stores.

The rotary-cranking style is easy to control and versatile. By turning a crank you set gears in motion to activate the bit at any speed you want. The drill chuck holds bits of many sizes and types. However, a quality model is nearly a foot long and weighs several pounds; it is bulky to store. It costs $8 or $9.

The push drill, generally less than a foot long and under a pound in weight, can be purchased for as little as $2. Forward or downward pressure on the handle activates an inner spiral, or ratchet, that turns the bit. Some have a reverse mechanism that al-

lows a bit to be backed out of a deep hole or one in which it is stuck.

SLIP-JOINT PLIERS

With this familiar household tool you can hold bolts while tightening nuts, grip small or slippery items, straighten nails, or cut wire. To help prevent injury, use pliers to grip broken glass or other sharp objects.

For general household use, choose a pair about 6 inches long with "combination" jaws. The outer jaws should be parallel and finely grooved for holding or bending small objects. The concave inner jaws should have rugged teeth for gripping round or squarish objects up to ¾ inch across when the slip joint is in the "open" position. At the extreme inside, the jaws should serve as shears for cutting wire.

Durable pliers are made of forged steel and have a bright, reflective finish or a blue-black sheen. Handles should be easy to grasp even when the jaws are wide open and should be cross-scored or knurled for nonslip gripping. The slip-joint fastener should be impossible to loosen without special tools. Such pliers cost $3 or less.

ADJUSTABLE WRENCH

To tighten or loosen nuts or bolts or other threaded parts, you need a wrench with an adjustable jaw. It is especially useful in plumbing work.

An 8-inch model, with an angled head and a spiral midsection for adjusting the jaw, will suit most household needs. Select one with a reflective finish or a blue-black sheen, a knurled spiral for easy turning, and a jaw with exactly parallel parts for good grasp. The handle should be comfortable to grip and have a hole at the end for hanging on a peg. Such a wrench costs about $4 or $5.

Chapter 4 • The Basic Toolbox

MEASURING TOOLS

The least expensive measures are the 6-foot tapes commonly used in sewing. Yardsticks are also readily available and moderately priced and are easier to use accurately, but they are not as conveniently stored as folding rules or steel tapes on reels.

A steel tape that is rigid when extended but flexible enough to retract into a small case is especially convenient if you work without a helper. A 10-foot model with a ½-inch blade is useful for most home purposes and costs about $4. The tape is marked in inches and 1/16-inch intervals and ends in a hook that holds onto objects being measured. The case should prevent the extended tape from turning over and should have measuring marks that can be read as an extension of the tape. Many cases have a friction lock to hold the tape at a desired length.

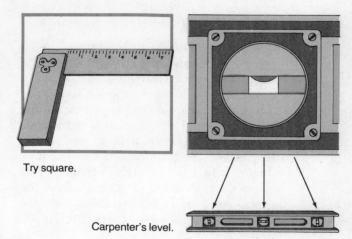
Try square.

Carpenter's level.

TRY SQUARE

The try square consists of two parts at right angles to each other: a thick wood or iron stock and a thin steel blade. Most try squares are made with the blades graduated in inches and fractions of an inch. The blade length varies from 2 to 12 inches. This tool is used for setting or checking lines or surfaces that have to be at right angles to each other. It costs about $3.

LEVEL

The level is a tool designed to determine whether a plane or surface is true horizontal or true vertical. It is a simple instrument consisting of a liquid, such as alcohol or chloroform, partially filling a glass vial or tube so that a bubble remains. The tube is mounted in a frame of aluminum or wood. Levels are equipped with one, two, or more tubes. One tube is built in the frame at right angles to another. The tube is slightly curved, causing the bubble to always seek the highest point in the tube. On the outside of the tube are two sets of graduation lines separated by a space. Leveling is accomplished when the air bubble is centered between the graduation lines.

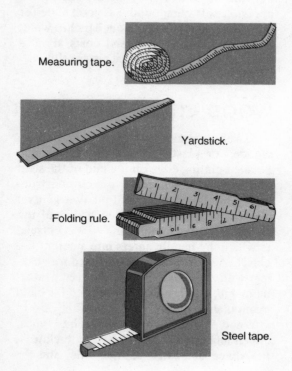
Measuring tape.

Yardstick.

Folding rule.

Steel tape.

HANDSAW

Handsaws designed for general cutting consist of ripsaws and crosscut saws. The major difference between a ripsaw and a crosscut saw is the shape of the teeth. Teeth with square-faced chisel-type cutting edges do a good job of cutting with the grain (called ripping), but a poor job of cutting across the grain (called crosscutting). Teeth with beveled, knife-type cutting edges do a good job of cutting across the grain, but a poor job of cutting with the grain. A quality handsaw costs $8 to $12.

NESTED SAW

For small cutting jobs, a nested saw with three interchangeable blades is a good choice. It can be stored compactly and costs about $5.

The narrow, tapered keyhole and compass blades, each about a foot long, make straight or curved cuts in wood; the compass style is particularly adapted to tight curves. The third blade has many small teeth for sawing through nails, wire, bone, or even frozen meat. The handle should be smooth hardwood or plastic with a comfortable grip and a device for securing the blades firmly.

UTILITY KNIFE

The small, sharp blade of the utility knife held firmly by a sturdy handle can save you time and effort in cutting twine, trimming carpet tile or wallpaper, and opening cartons. It is specially designed to lessen the chance of cutting accidents during handyman jobs and is an excellent safety investment for your toolbox.

Look for a utility knife with a single-edge, replaceable blade held secure by a screw at the throat of the handle. The handle should be shaped to fit your hand and hollow for the storage of extra blades. Some handles have a push-button to retract the blade or extend it for conveniently cutting different thicknesses. Such a knife costs about $2.

PUTTY KNIFE

A putty knife helps you attain a smooth finish when spreading spackling compound into chipped spots or small holes in walls, applying putty to window frames, or inserting grout between tiles. It can also be used for minor scraping of paint, plaster, or adhesive.

The thin, polished blade should have a blunt end and no sharp edges; it should be firmly attached to the handle by two rivets or eyelets. Stiffer blades are best for scraping; the more flexible ones are handy for applying soft compounds. A good style for general use has a blade about 3 inches wide, is about 7 inches long, and costs about a dollar. Narrower blades are also useful.

WOOD CHISEL

A wood chisel is a steel tool fitted with a wooden or plastic handle. It has a single beveled cutting edge on the end of the steel part, or blade. According to their construction, chisels are divided into two general classes: tang chisels, in which part of the chisel enters the handle, and socket chisels, in which the handle enters into a part of the chisel. A socket chisel is designed for striking with a wooden mallet (never a steel hammer); a tang chisel is designed for hand manipulation only.

Wood chisels are also divided into types, depending upon their weight and thickness, the shape or design of the blade, and the

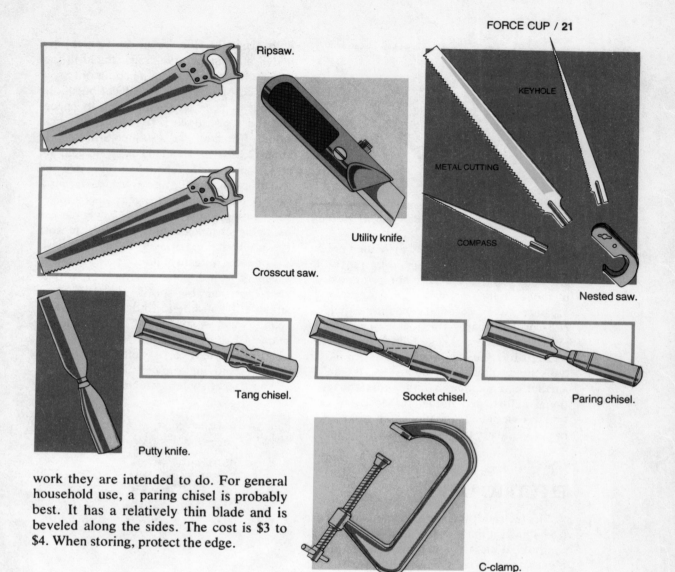

Ripsaw.

Utility knife.

KEYHOLE

METAL CUTTING

COMPASS

Nested saw.

Crosscut saw.

Tang chisel.

Socket chisel.

Paring chisel.

Putty knife.

C-clamp.

work they are intended to do. For general household use, a paring chisel is probably best. It has a relatively thin blade and is beveled along the sides. The cost is $3 to $4. When storing, protect the edge.

C-CLAMP

Named for the shape of its frame, the C-clamp holds work in place or presses two pieces together for gluing. It is handy when you use adhesive to repair furniture or objects made of metal or plastic.

A 6-inch, light-duty type with an extra-deep opening can accommodate fairly large items but adjusts by means of a screw for smaller work. A sliding handle turns the screw to tighten the clamp, and a swivel button prevents the screw end from marring the work surface. For many jobs you will need a pair. They cost $6 or $7.

FORCE CUP

Aptly called "the plumber's helper," a force cup is the well-known tool of first defense against clogged sink or bathtub drains

Bell-shaped force cup.

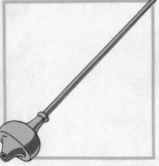

Ball-shaped force cup.

and overflowing toilets. By providing pressure and suction into stopped-up pipes, it can help you avoid water damage or costly plumber's bills.

Force cups are available with either a bell- or ball-shaped flexible cup screwed onto a wood handle. A ball-shaped style with a 2-foot handle is satisfactory for most households and costs about $3. It has a smaller end opening than the more conventional bell-shaped model for easier insertion in toilet discharge pipes, but it can also be conveniently used on drains.

ELECTRIC DRILL

An electric drill can do so many jobs that it is almost a must in the do-it-yourselfer's toolbox. With it you can make holes in almost any material. By using its accessories and attachments you can sand, polish, grind, buff, stir paint, and drive screws.

Depending on quality, size, gearing, and special features, a drill for home use costs from $5 to $50 or more. Your best choice is a model with the work capacity and special features you regularly use. The work capacity of a drill depends on its chuck size and rated revolutions per minute (RPM).

The chuck size is the diameter of the largest bit shank that the drill chuck can hold. Home-use sizes are ¼, ⅜, and ½

inch. Usually, the larger the chuck, the wider and deeper the holes the drill can bore; ¼-inch drills are most common.

The RPM rating is an indication of the number of gear sets in a model, its speed, and the type of work for which it is best suited. For example, a ¼-inch drill rated at about 2,000 RPM usually has one gear set and is appropriate for rapid drilling in wood and use with sanding and polishing accessories. A model with more gears has a lower RPM rating and works more slowly but can make bigger holes in hard metals or masonry without stalling or overheating.

For most jobs around a home, a single-speed drill is adequate. However, a two-speed or variable-speed model is more suitable if you intend to drill material that requires a slow speed or if you want to use many accessories. A drill with both variable speed and reverse is effective for driving and removing screws.

The trigger switch, which starts the drill,

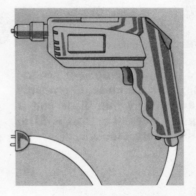

Electric drill.

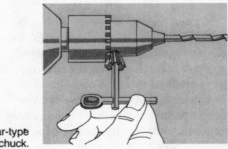

Gear-type drill chuck.

is on the pistol-grip handle, and many models include a switch lock for continuous operation. You activate the lock by pressing a button; the lock instantly releases if you tighten your squeeze on the trigger switch.

Variable-speed drills have trigger switches that allow you to vary bit speed from almost nothing up to maximum RPM by trigger-finger pressure. Some have controls that allow you to preset the maximum RPM for each operation.

Drills with reverse have separate reverse controls in different positions, depending on the brand. To protect the motor, allow the drill to come to a full stop before reversing direction.

The front of the drill, where bits and other accessories are inserted and removed, is called the chuck. The three-jaw gear type is the most common. Its collar is first hand-closed on the shank of a bit. Then a key is inserted into the chuck body and turned to tighten the three jaws simultaneously and with considerable force. Some models have a holder to make key loss less likely.

Some "bargain" drills have chucks that are hand-tightened by means of knurled collars. They may either offer a poor hold on bits and accessories during work or be difficult to loosen when work is finished.

Examine chuck placement as well as quality. The higher the chuck on the front of the housing, the easier the drill will be to use in corners.

DRILL ACCESSORIES

The manufacturer's catalog will contain information on the accessories available for particular drill brands and models. The common accessories that enable you to use an electric drill for many different jobs are described here.

A drill bit has a working end that makes holes and a smooth shank that is grasped by the jaws of a chuck. Although bits can be bought individually, they cost less if purchased in sets.

The twist bit, the most commonly used, cuts cylindrical holes. It has a sharp point and two spiral-shaped cutting edges that lift chips out of the hole as the bit turns. Carbon steel twist bits are suited to drilling wood and soft metals; high-speed steel bits cut wood, soft metals, and mild steel; tungsten carbide or carbide-tipped bits cut hard metals and masonry. Cutting diameters commonly range from 1/16 to ½ inch.

The spade bit cuts large cylindrical holes in wood. It has a flat, spade-shaped driving end with a pointed tip. Common cutting diameters range from ⅜ inch to 1 inch.

The wood-screw pilot bit has three widths of cutting edge. The narrowest drills a hole to give screw threads solid anchorage. The next makes a shaft for the unthreaded screw shank. The widest makes a hole, or countersink, for flat-headed

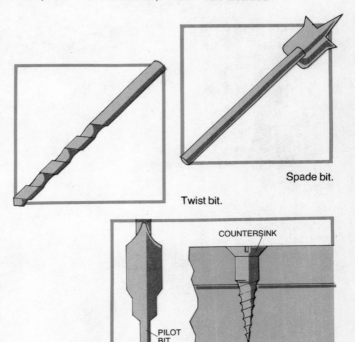

Spade bit.

Twist bit.

COUNTERSINK

PILOT BIT

Pilot bit.

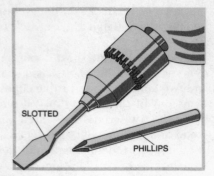

Screw-driving bit.

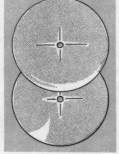

Sanding disc.

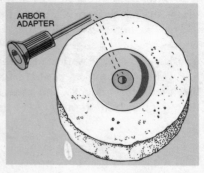

Grinding wheel.

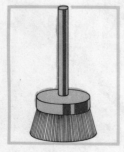

Wire brush disc.

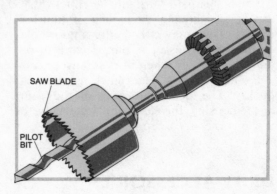

Hole saw.

screws. A detachable stop can make shallow or deep countersinks.

The screw-driving bit attaches to drills with variable speed and reverse to drive and remove slotted and Phillips-head screws. On single- or two-speed drills, the bit must be used with a screw-driving attachment.

Polishing and sanding discs, grinding wheels, wire-brush discs, and hole saws are usually secured to a drill by an arbor that goes through the center hole of the wheel or disc and is fastened by a washer and nut or by a screw and washer. A flange keeps the wheel from slipping down the shank that fits into the drill chuck.

Discs are used with either abrasive paper for sanding or a soft bonnet for polishing. Grinding wheels are for sharpening tools or smoothing metal. Wire brushes remove paint, rust, and dirt from wood and metal. Hole saws cut round holes through boards or sheet materials by means of a rim saw blade and a centered pilot bit. Common diameters range from ½ inch to 4 inches.

5

Floors and Stairs

SQUEAKS EMANATING from floors and stairs are a grudgingly accepted annoyance in most households. Few people, however, realize that, aside from their exacerbating effects on nerves, squeaks can signal the impending doom of a structure—or at least a greater problem than mere annoyance. Floor and stair squeaks are often symptoms of far more serious examples of house frame deterioration.

Squeaks caused by a sagging floor may indicate a weakness in the floor's understructure. Age, the settling of the foundation, the shifting or addition of heavy loads, and perhaps even poorly planned renovation of rooms can all create stresses to the beams and joists that support the flooring. Caught in time, many of these problems can be handled by the homeowner before they demand a thorough overhaul that would require professional help.

Often an old floor can be corrected and made like new with only some simple labor on your part. Resilient floor coverings such as linoleum, vinyl, or tile can be installed, or the existing surface material can be repaired, at relatively little cost. Concrete flooring may betray the effects of poor workmanship or corrosion—you should be familiar with the signs and know how to go about repairing the damage or stopping it in its tracks.

WOOD FLOORS

Why live with a floor that complains all the time? Elimination of squeaks and creaks can be managed with relatively little effort, the means depending on the floor's construction and whether the subflooring is accessible from below.

Most wood floors consist of two layers: a subfloor of boards or plywood and the finished floor of narrower boards—usually hardwood—tongued and grooved together and nailed into place. The subflooring is supported from underneath by wood joists normally spaced on 16-inch centers. A squeak is usually the result of a board or

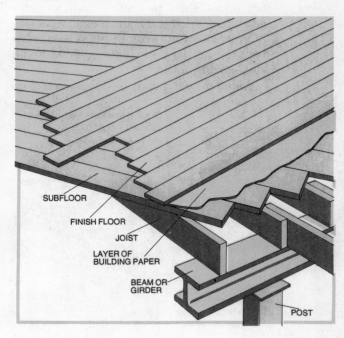

SUBFLOOR

FINISH FLOOR

JOIST

LAYER OF
BUILDING PAPER

BEAM OR
GIRDER

POST

Wood floor construction.

boards having separated from what is beneath. The finish floor may have pulled away from the subfloor, or the subfloor may have warped or sagged and pulled away from the joists.

It is best to make your inspection and repairs from under the floor, if this is not concealed by a ceiling or other barrier. Have someone walk around overhead so that you can pinpoint the problem. Inspect the area around the squeak. Make sure joists are level, and check between joists and subflooring for signs of warping or lifting of the floorboards.

If a squeak is detected directly over a joist, an effective method of quieting it is to drive thin wood shims between the joist and subflooring. Pieces of shingle are ideal for this. Hammer them into place over one or more joists. as necessary. Larger wedges of wood can be used if needed.

▲ When the squeak originates between joists, first install a header of 2 x 4 or 2 x 6 lumber to act as a base for the shimming. Cut the header so that it fits snugly between two joists. Tap it up firmly against the subfloor, narrow edge up, and toenail it securely in place. Now work in shims as needed between header and subfloor. This should eliminate the noise.

Another approach is to drive a screw up

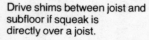
Drive shims between joist and subfloor if squeak is directly over a joist.

Install header if squeak originates between joists.

Drill pilot hole through subfloor.

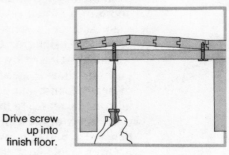
Drive screw up into finish floor.

through the subfloor and into the finish floor where the squeak is found. Use a wood screw about 1 inch long for this operation—enough to penetrate the subfloor but not the finish floor—and have someone stand on the floor overhead. It is best to drill a pilot hole to help start the screw and to avoid splitting the hardwood floor. Again, be careful not to penetrate the finish floor. Maintain the weight overhead as you drive the screw so that subfloor and finish floor will be brought together.

These methods cannot be used if the understructure is inaccessible. In that case, you will have to make the repairs from topside. You can often silence a squeak by working some talcum powder or powdered stainless lubricant into the cracks between floorboards, but this is only a temporary treatment. The best way is to nail the noisy board.

▲ Use long finishing nails for this job. Drive them in pairs, as required, along or across the board. The nails should be driven at an angle, each pair forming a V, with the points meeting under the subfloor. Drill

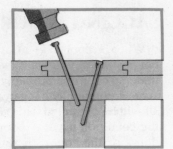

Drive in
finishing nails.

Set, fill holes
with putty.

pilot holes to avoid splitting the hardwood. Use a nailset to recess nailheads. The holes can be filled with putty or plugged with wax patching crayon. If you are doing this kind of work on a floor that is covered with linoleum or tile, about the only thing you can do is nail right through the floor covering. A lot of guesswork is involved here because the boards are unseen, so prod around with your foot to try to pinpoint the squeak as closely as possible. This will avoid having to drive too many nails. The holes in the covering can be plugged with wax crayon.

CRACKED AND SPLIT FLOORING

Floorboards become damaged for a variety of reasons, the most common of which are shrinkage and expansion because of exposure to water. When wet, the boards expand against their joints. As they dry, they return to their former size, causing cracks to appear either between the joints or along the grain of the board. New floors laid with green or wet wood also produce cracks.

You should make it a rule never to wash a wood floor with water. Rather, treat the wood with an application of any of the floor sealers available, then give it a good waxing for an easy-to-maintain protective finish. If you use a polyurethane finish on the floor, waxing is not recommended. This durable finish is maintained by simply wiping it clean with a cloth or mop.

Cracks can be filled with a variety of compounds. You can use a mixture of glue and sawdust, a wood-fiber putty, or plastic wood. The compound is pressed into the crack and then sanded and stained to the proper color. You can also fashion small wedges of hardwood to fill the crack, hammering them in tightly, then planing the excess and sanding smooth.

Splits along the grain of a board should be filled with a mixture of glue and sawdust to prevent the board from splitting further.

A warped board can sometimes be

Fill cracks.

Drive wedges into cracks.

Planing a warped floorboard.

Nailing warped board flat.

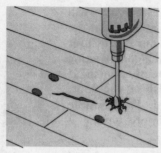

1. Drill holes in corners of damaged board.

2. Chisel out damaged section across and along its grain.

3. Remove damaged section of board.

4. Nail new piece in place and countersink the nails.

evened off with a good sanding or by planing. First make sure all nailheads have been recessed. If the board is a wide one, you can also try to flatten it by soaking it with water, then nailing it flat. Otherwise it will have to be replaced wth a new board.

▲To remove a badly worn or damaged section of board, first drill large holes at each end of the damaged section, The holes should not extend through the subfloor below. Drill close to the edges of the board, then carefully chisel out the damaged section across and along its grain, taking care not to harm the tongue and groove sides of the adjoining boards. Cut the replacement piece to size. Using a chisel, remove the bottom half of the groove on the replacement piece. You can now slip the new board into place, nail it down, countersink the nailheads, and plane it flush if necessary.

SAGGING FLOORS

When a floor sags at any point or feels bouncy when you walk over it, part of the understructure is probably weak. This presents a potentially dangerous condition that should be corrected without delay. Because the condition usually is found on the lower floors of the house, thereby providing you with ready access to the understructure, you can often make the necessary repairs and adjustments yourself.

The cause of the sagging may be that the joists are spaced too far apart to provide rigid support for weakened subflooring. One or more joists may have warped or sagged. The beam that supports the joists may not be making contact all the way across.

▲Use a long straightedge and level as you inspect the subflooring, joists, and supporting beams. If a joist has warped or sagged but is otherwise sound, you can raise the floor by driving hardwood wedges between the joist and subflooring. Additional support is gained by toenailing a sturdy crosspiece between the joists under the floor.

Check to see that all joists are resting on the main beam. It often happens that a beam sags at the center—particularly if it is made of wood. Support posts may be spaced too far apart, or they may have buckled or rotted or sunk into the concrete floor. Or they may be absent altogether, in which case you will have to add one or more new posts.

■Adjustable metal posts that have a screw-type jack at the end can be used to raise the beam into position. These can be left in place as permanent supports, if needed. The base of the jack must rest on a solid cement footing. If the cement floor is less than 4 inches thick or shows signs of deterioration, you must put in a new footing.

■Because of potential damage to the frame and walls of the house, you must never at-

Chapter 5 • Floors and Stairs

tempt to raise the beam more than a slight amount at a time. Put the jack post into position under the beam so that it just touches. Make sure the jack is perfectly vertical, then give the screw a half turn and stop. Wait several days to a week, then give it another half turn. Do not be in a hurry—chances are it took quite a while for the beam to sag that much, so it can wait to be straightened out. Continue a little at a time until the floor overhead is level, then either insert a chock between the existing post and the beam or leave the jack post in position permanently.

You can check the level of the floor with a long straightedge as you go along. Or you can tack a string from wall to wall across the floor above the sag. If the string is kept taut, you will be able to observe the distance between it and the floor as this distance gradually diminishes.

CONCRETE FLOORS

Smooth-finish concrete flooring is durable and normally requires little maintenance. Trouble can sometimes arise, however, generally as the result of poor workmanship. Because of its porosity, new concrete should be treated with an application of penetrating varnish or paint sealer. A paste-wax coating can be added for further protection.

Concrete sealer paints can also be applied to correct pitted and dusty concrete, two common problems. These paints come in clear form and in colors with silicone, epoxy-resin, or latex bases, the last a good choice for rooms that experience occasional dampness. It is usually necessary to apply more than one coat of paint—the first to seal and the following to fill.

Keep an eye out for damp spots on slab floors that have heating or water pipes imbedded in the concrete; this may indicate

Use wedge to raise subfloor.

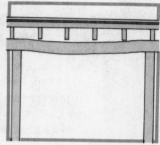

Sagging beam.

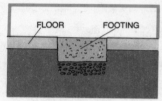

Footing for post.

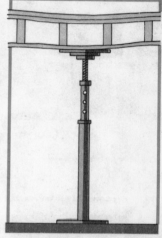

Place jack post in position.

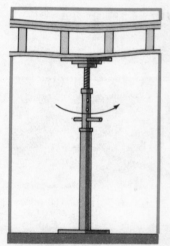

Give jack a
half-turn at a time.

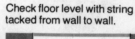

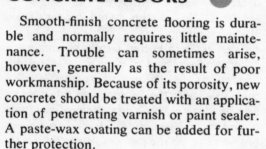

Check floor level with
long straightedge.

Check floor level with string
tacked from wall to wall.

a leak in the pipe and the need to call in professional help. Simple cracks can be filled easily enough with patching compound, then treated as described previously. If a floor is badly damaged, however, a reinforced topping of concrete is needed. This is a job for the professionals. An unsightly floor that is still sound can be prepared to receive a covering of tile or linoleum.

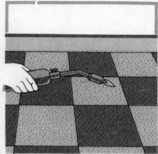

1. Loosening tile with electric iron or with torch.

2. Prying up the tile.

3. Cut around tile edges.

4. Chisel tile.

5. Scrape old cement.

TILE AND SHEET FLOORING

Resilient floor coverings laid over wood and concrete are cemented in place with an adhesive such as mastic. Kept waxed and clean, they wear well, but after a time it will become necessary to replace one or more damaged tiles or deal with worn or broken sheet flooring. A seam may also come unstuck, in which case a recementing job is needed.

Finding a replacement floor tile that matches the rest is not always easy. Manufacturers of tile recommend that extra pieces be purchased with the original floor, not only to allow for wastage during installation, but to provide for just this contingency. If you are really stuck with a floor pattern, style, or color that is not available, a possible solution would be to remove several good tiles and install new ones that will create a limited pattern or decorative path encompassing the damaged area. Of course, you should first check with your dealer to see whether the tile might be available through the manufacturer. Take along a sample.

Tiles are laid butted tightly against each other, and removal of one, if not carefully done, can cause damage to others. To make the job easier, the cement and the tile can first be softened by heat. The professionals have special "hot plates" for this purpose, but you can do the job almost as effectively with a household electric iron. Set it to its hottest and put a damp cloth between it and the tile. A propane torch played over the center of the tile is a faster method, but the flame should not come in direct contact with the tile.

While the tile is still hot, work the tip of a putty knife under a raised corner or seam and carefully pry it loose. If it does not come easily—or if you are unable to use heat because of the tile's composition—you may have to cut out the tile in pieces with a

Install
new tile.

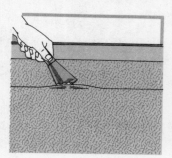

Apply adhesive
under seam.

Slit "bubble."

Work adhesive
under lifted area.

hammer and chisel, taking care not to gouge the subfloor. Begin this operation by first cutting into the seam around the tile with a sharp knife. As you remove the tile with the chisel, work from the center out to the edges; this minimizes the possibility of damage to surrounding tiles.

Sometimes, if the damaged tile is removed in one piece by the heating method, the cement is tacky enough so that you can simply press a new tile in place. Otherwise, the old cement should be scraped off to provide a smooth base, then new cement put down. Apply it evenly and sparingly to avoid its squeezing up around the edges of the tile.

On linoleum and sheet vinyl, a seam may lift because the cement was not applied properly or has been weakened by water. This can be corrected by applying fresh cement to the area beneath the flooring material and placing a heavy object on top until it dries. Work the cement in with a flexible blade, taking care not to tear the material. Wipe off the excess and allow plenty of time for drying. If there is a bubble or

raised spot remote from a seam, slit the raised portion along its length with a razor or sharp knife and work the cement under the lifted areas.

You can renew worn or grubby-looking linoleum, if it is otherwise intact, by giving it a few coats of floor enamel in a color of your choice. First prepare the floor by removing all traces of wax or grease; steel wool and alcohol will help here. When it is clean and dry, apply a first coat of paint. When that is dry, give it a finish coat. You can add more colors to provide a stipple effect or to create a pattern laid out with masking tape. The floor should then be waxed to protect the enamel.

Broken linoleum can be repaired with a patch of new material. Tape the new linoleum over the damaged surface and cut through both new and old linoleum with a sharp knife. A straightedge will help guide the cut. The material is more flexible and lies flat better if it is warm. Remove the old piece and check the fit of the cut patch. Trim the surrounding linoleum so that there is a 1/16-inch gap all around—this will fill in

1. Lay new linoleum patch over damaged area; cut both at once.

2. Trim around cut area.

3. Press patch in place.

4. Tap seams flush.

later when the new piece swells naturally. Apply cement and press the patch in place. The seams can be tapped flush with a mallet or a hammer and a block of wood.

Sheet flooring and tile can be applied

Fill, smooth cracks in concrete floor.

Make a pattern for sheet flooring (at right).

Trace onto sheet material (far right).

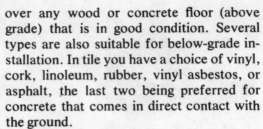

over any wood or concrete floor (above grade) that is in good condition. Several types are also suitable for below-grade installation. In tile you have a choice of vinyl, cork, linoleum, rubber, vinyl asbestos, or asphalt, the last two being preferred for concrete that comes in direct contact with the ground.

Before tile can be put down, any irregularities in the floor must be corrected. Make sure nailheads do not protrude. Sand or plane smooth any raised surfaces and eliminate any existing squeaks. If it is a concrete floor, fill any cracks or gouges.

Keep in mind that resilient tiles of any composition will conform to the shape of the surface they cover. If the floor is uneven, broken, badly scarred, or pitted, you will have to lay in a hard, flat foundation for the tiles. This layer can be of hardboard or plywood, and it is fastened directly to the existing flooring. If a concrete floor is subject to persistent dampness, condensation, or leakage, correct this before proceeding any further, either by laying a waterproof barrier or pouring a new topping.

Tile can be applied successfully by the do-it-yourselfer, but the directions supplied by the manufacturer must be followed to the letter. Otherwise the results can be disappointing. Your dealer can advise you as to the number of tiles you will need to cover a given area and also give specific recommendations for the make or type of tile. When laying sheet flooring, first make a pattern of taped-together newspaper or

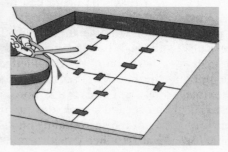

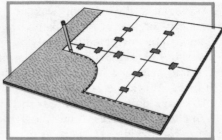

heavy wrapping paper, using small pieces to fit around corners and obstructions. Use this to trace an outline for cutting on the sheet (remembering to turn the pattern over). It is a quick, simple step that can prevent a lot of irritation.

STAIR REPAIRS

Most stairs consist of three sections: tread, riser, and stringer. On some stairs the tread rests on the riser in a simple butt joint of glue and nails; in others a dado-and-rabbet joint or simple dado is used. The stringers or side pieces serve to support the treads.

●When squeaks occur, it is because the tread or riser has worked loose at some point. If the treads are attached by butt joints (you can check this by prying off a part of the molding under the nose of the tread), you can tighten the tread by renailing it to the top of the riser. Have someone stand on the tread during the operation. Drive finishing nails at angles through the top of the tread into the center of the riser top. The holes can be filled with wood putty. If the tread is made of hardwood, you can avoid splits and bent nails by first drilling pilot holes.

▲On a dadoed or dado-and-rabbet setup, you can avoid nailing by removing the molding and working small glued wedges into the side of the tread slot. If the underside of the stairway is accessible, apply the wedges from behind. While under there, check for any loose wedges betweeen the tread and stringer. Tighten these or replace them, as necessary.

■Replacement of a damaged or broken tread is a job that usually calls for the services of a carpenter. However, if the wall end of the tread butts against the stringer, rather than being recessed into it, the job is considerably easier and you may wish to tackle it yourself.

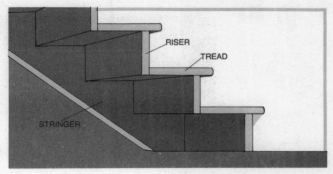

Stair construction: treads rest on a riser in simple butt joint.

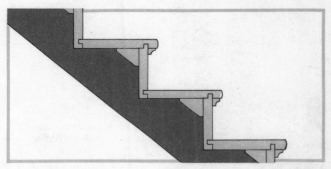

Stair construction: tread is rabbeted and dadoed.

Renail tread to riser to eliminate squeak (right).

Working wedges into rabbet, avoiding nailing (below).

Wedging from behind stair (below right).

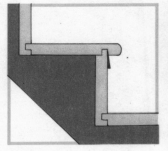

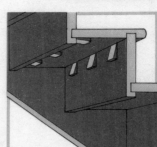

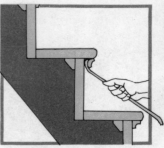

1. Remove molding from under the tread nosing.

2. Use hacksaw to loosen bottom of baluster.

3. Twist loose top of baluster from the anchor.

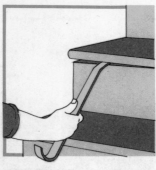

4. Loosen tread from riser by prying under the nosing.

5. Use old tread as pattern for new step.

Flip tread over to other side if wear is the only problem.

First remove all molding from under the tread nosing. The feet of the balusters may be toenailed to the top of the tread or glued into slots. In such cases, use a hacksaw blade to sever the balusters as close to the tread as possible, exercising care to limit damage while cutting. The tops of the balusters are usually held in place with glue and can be separated from the anchor by twisting.

Hammer carefully under the nosing of the tread until there is a gap between the tread and riser. A pry bar may help here. Depending on the construction of the stair, you can continue prying until the tread can be worked loose by hand, or you can cut the nails that hold it with a hacksaw. The tread can now be used as a pattern for the new step. Or, if wear is the only problem, it may be possible to turn the tread over and use the other side. Fasten the tread with glue and nails; fill the nail holes with wood putty and sand smooth.

6

Walls and Ceilings

A<small>T ONE POINT</small> or another, every homeowner and apartment dweller is faced with the problem of correcting damage to ceilings and walls. The damage may have been caused by an external malignant force (such as little Junior perfecting his curve ball indoors, using the wall as a backstop), or it may have occurred because the house is settling (as all houses do).

Whatever the cause and wherever the blame may lie, damaged walls and ceilings detract from the beauty, as well as the value, of a home. Fortunately, most minor wall and ceiling maladies can be remedied by the layperson with a little time to spare. The tools and materials needed for these jobs are often on hand or are cheaply and easily available.

PLASTER REPAIRS

Plaster on ceilings and walls is generally applied over a lathing of wood, metal, or gypsumboard, the latter most common except in older homes. This lathing serves as a foundation for the plaster and is in turn fixed to the framework behind it.

Small cracks and holes in plaster can be filled with spackling compound, which is available in either dry or premixed form. First clear away all loose plaster and dust. Work the spackle tightly into the opening with a flexible putty knife. Trim the excess flush with the wall, wiping with the knife in alternate crisscross strokes. Give the compound plenty of time to dry, then sand the area smooth, using medium sandpaper.

GYPSUM WALLBOARD

Gypsum wallboard is a surfacing material commonly used for both walls and ceilings. Also known as plasterboard and Sheetrock (a trade name), it is made of compressed

gypsum plaster between two sheets of heavy paper or cardboard. The sheets range in sizes up to 4 by 16 feet, though 4

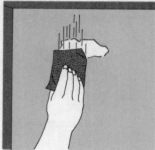

To repair small cracks in plaster, work spackle into cracks (left) and sand area smooth (right).

by 8 sheets are most favored by builders, and come in thicknesses of ⅜ and ½ inch.

Gypsum wallboard is usually nailed (or cemented and nailed) directly to the framing studs. The board is subject to dents, such as may be caused by the sharp corner of a piece of furniture. Depressions of this sort can be corrected with spackling compound or a special gypsum cement. Nail

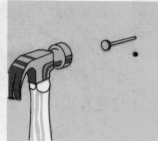

1. Popped nail (above left).

2. Drive in new nail (above right).

3. Drive nail below surface (left).

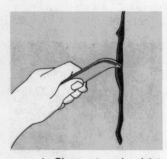

1. Clean out crack or joint.

2. Apply spackle.

3. Apply tape.

4. Apply more spackle.

5. Sand smooth after the spackle is dry.

holes can be filled in this fashion also. No preparation of the surface is necessary, and the compound can be smoothed with sandpaper when it is dry.

Settling of the house's foundation or the use of green wood for backing supports can result in a vertical warping of the wallboard. When this happens, the nails that hold the panel in place may "pop" loose. This can be corrected by removing the loosened nail and driving a single nail just above or below the old nail hole, at the same time pushing the board firmly to hold it in place. Use only a screw-type nail for the fastening, and hammer it carefully so that a shallow depression is formed around the nailhead. Patch and finish the repair with spackling compound.

The joints between panels are closed with gypsum cement and a special reinforcing tape. To close a seam that has broken open, first clean out the seam with a sharp-pointed tool (a pre-pop-top beer-can opener does a good job). Pull or scrape away remnants of the old tape, then sand the seam to prepare the surface. The area you have sanded should be slightly wider than the replacement tape.

Using a broad knife with a 4-inch blade, lay the cement smoothly and evenly into the seam and around it. Before the cement has had time to dry, apply the tape over the seam, centering it and removing all wrinkles and air bubbles with the blade of the knife. Now apply more cement over the tape. Work it on smoothly, and remove all excess. After it dries, sand it smooth. To

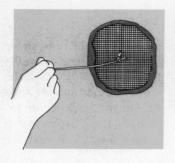

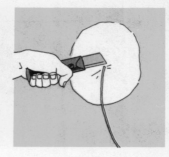

Tie string to mesh, insert in hole (far left).

Hold string, apply spackle (center).

Snip off string, finish (left).

provide a smoother finish, it may be necessary to apply another coat of cement and repeat the sanding.

Since a hole in wallboard is "bottomless" because of the absence of backing, you cannot simply work patching compound into it and expect it to hold. To repair a hole, cut a piece of wire mesh a bit larger than the hole. Tie a string near the center of the mesh and work the mesh through the hole until it covers the opening from behind. Maintain a grip on the string while applying spackle to within ⅛ inch of the surface. Give the compound a chance to set, snip off the excess string, and carefully finish off the surface.

If a large section of wallboard must be replaced, you must provide backing for the new section. Use a straightedge to draw parallel lines above and below the damaged area. With a keyhole saw, cut carefully along the lines until you encounter the studs on either side of the damage. Cut another inch of wallboard so that you are over the center line of the stud. Now cut straight down along this line on both studs. If the damaged area extends beyond the width of two studs, it is best to continue the horizontal cut to the next stud.

Measure the size of the opening and cut a new piece of board to fit. You do not have to use a saw; use a sharp knife to score the face of the board. Snap it over a straightedge or the edge of a table, then score the rear to break it off cleanly. The new section can be nailed directly to the studs, but first

you must provide horizontal backing because of the horizontal seams. Use sections of 2 x 4 or 2 x 3 lumber, sawing them to size

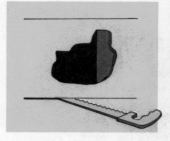
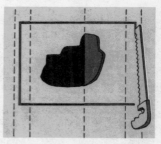

1. Cut damaged area horizontally.   2. Cut along ends over studs.

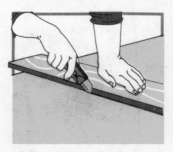
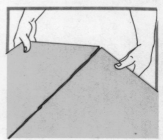

3. Score face of new board.   4. Snap the board.

5. Score back.   6. Provide horizontal backing.

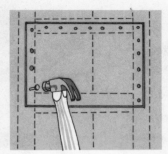

7. Nail new section in place.

so they can be toenailed to the studs. One support for the top and bottom of the replacement section will suffice. Nail the section into place and finish the seams as described above.

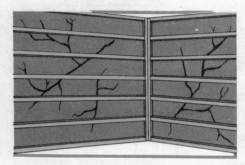

Apply furring over plaster wall.

Check furring for plumb (true vertical).

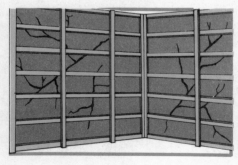

Frame for furring over uneven concrete wall.

WALL PANELING

Unsightly wall surfaces can be refinished with paneling of your choice, such as wallboard, plywood, fiberboard, or hardboard, which come in various finishes and require no further covering. Or you may decide to panel a wall with wood. It all depends on the application and how much you wish to spend.

In all cases, though, you have to provide a base to support the new material. This is normally done with furring strips, lengths of 1 x 2 lumber that can be purchased at your local lumberyard.

To apply furring to a plaster wall, the strips must be placed horizontally and nailed to the wall studs. Spacing is usually 16 inches on center. Some types of paneling also require vertical furring strips where two panels meet; follow the manufacturer's recommendations in this regard. The baseboard along the bottom of the wall should be removed, as well as any molding and trim. Openings in the wall, such as windows and doors, should be surrounded by furring strips. A long straightedge board can be used to detect bulges or depressions between the wall and the furring strips. A depression can be corrected by placing wood shims behind a strip to bring it in line with the others. A bulge is handled by planing the surface of the strip. Make these checks accurately—any variances will show plainly when the paneling is in place.

On concrete walls, the furring can be nailed directly, using special masonry nails. If the surface of a masonry wall is extremely irregular along its face, you should first nail up a framework of 2 x 2 lumber, shimming where necessary to even it up. Apply the furring over this.

When working with large sheets of light, flexible paneling, it is best to nail from the center out to the sides. This will avoid any buckling problem. Adhesive may also be used—check the manufacturer's recommendations. When measuring how much paneling you need to cover the area, allow 10 percent extra for waste.

CERAMIC TILE

Ceramic tile is usually set in place with a white, waterproof tile calking used to fill the spaces around the tile. These same adhesive compounds can be used to make repairs on ceramic tile that has been cemented with portland cement, the old method of fastening.

As soon as a tile comes loose or cracks, it should be replaced. Use a chisel to cut around the damaged tile. Try not to damage the surrounding tiles. If the original fastening is cement, you will have to chisel away a part of the cement so that the replacement tile does not extend beyond the surface of the surrounding tiles.

Apply a generous bead of cement to the back of the new tile, then press it firmly into place. Wipe off all excess cement immediately. To hold the tile in place until the cement sets, support it with strips of masking tape. There should be an even space all around the tile. When the cement dries, remove the tape and fill the joints with white compound.

To cut ceramic tile to fit requires a glass cutter. Make a score along a guideline on the face of the tile, then place the tile over a nail and apply pressure on both sides to snap it clean. A file or emery cloth can be used to smooth the edge of the cut. For a curved cut, score the guideline, then make crisscross scores inside the area of the cut. Use a pliers to break out the scored section little by little.

When small, fine cracks appear in a ceramic tile the only cure is replacement. Shrinkage cracks around the wall of the tile can be filled with white plastic compound

1. Chisel around damaged tile.

2. Chisel cement backing.

3. Apply cement to new tile.

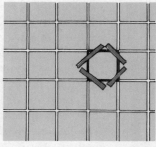

4. Support it while cement dries.

5. Fill joints with compound.

Score tile with glass cutter.

Snap over nail.

Making a curved cut.

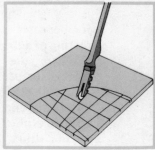

sold for that purpose. Correct such cracks as soon as they appear to prevent splash water or condensation from ruining the wall interior. Tile surfaces should never be cleaned with an abrasive agent. Warm water and a detergent are best (soap leaves a film on the tile).

CEILING TILE

Tiles are an excellent choice for many ceiling resurfacing jobs. Acoustical tile is especially popular, easy to work with, and can do much to brighten up a ceiling. It comes in a wide variety of patterns to suit just about any decor.

●Ceiling tile installation is begun at a room corner. However, since most rooms are slightly out of square or otherwise irregular, first find the center point of the ceiling by finding the midpoint on each of two opposite walls and stringing a line between these points; measure to the center of this line and describe a line at right angles to it. Measure from this center point to the walls to find the width of border tiles. In this way, if a tile must be cut to fit against the wall, it will be the same width at each side of the room, giving a balanced appearance.

●If an existing ceiling is level and in sound condition, ceiling tiles can be applied right over it with adhesive. Make sure the ceiling is clean and free of grease and water-soluble paint. Dab the back of each tile with adhesive in four or five spots and place it against the ceiling in approximate position, then slide it into place, spreading the adhesive. Slight depressions in the ceiling can be compensated for by applying a thicker coating of adhesive.

Where the existing ceiling is badly cracked or peeling, and in basements, attics, and other areas where the joists or rafters are exposed, the best method of installing ceiling tiles is by stapling them to furring strips. Place the first strip against the wall, nailing it securely to each joist.

The placement of the second strip depends upon the width you have determined for the border tiles. All other strips are placed on 12-inch centers (or whatever other width of tiles you may be using). Where pipes and cables are hung below the joists, a double layer of furring strips may be used to clear these obstructions. In this case, the first layer of strips may be spaced on about 24-inch centers (more or less, depending on where the obstructions fall). Pipes that are several inches below the joists should be boxed with furring strips. It is good insurance to make a sketch of your plumbing system, including the locations of valves, before enclosure so that a minimum number of tiles need be removed if you ever require access to the pipes.

The furring strips should be checked with a level and shimmed with wood wedges where necessary to provide an even, level backing for the tiles. Snap a chalk line across the furring strips as a guideline for border tiles. Measure and cut each border tile individually to assure an accurate fit. (When measuring, do not include tongues and flanges.) Cut the tiles face up with a sharp fiberboard knife. Fit the first tile in the corner, carefully aligning it with the two intersecting guidelines; staple it securely through the flanges. Install the border tiles adjacent to the corner tile, then install another border tile along each wall and begin filling in between the border tiles with full tiles, working across the ceiling. Make certain that each tile is butted tightly to and aligned properly with its neighbors before stapling. Wherever possible, light fixtures, vents, and other ceiling fittings should be positioned between furring strips so they fall in the center of a single tile, minimizing cutting and fitting. When you reach the borders on the opposite side of the room, the final tiles are face-nailed to the furring strips. A cove or crown molding at the joint between walls and ceiling conceals the nails.

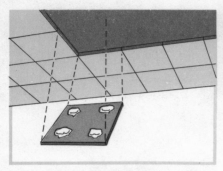

Using mastic to install ceiling tile.

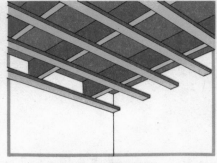

Furring for ceiling tile.

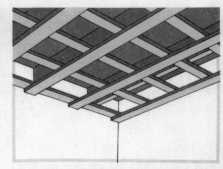

Double layer of strips to lower ceiling.

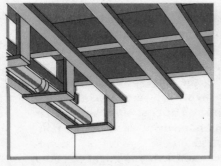

Box around obstructions.

Check furring for evenness.

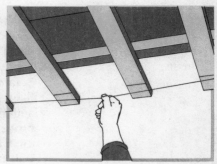

Snap a chalk guideline.

Cutting tile.

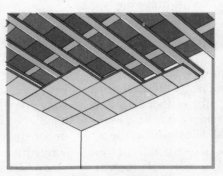

Installing tile ceiling.

Tile around ceiling fixture.

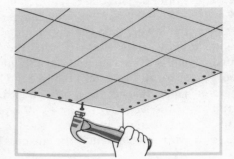

Nail final tiles to furring.

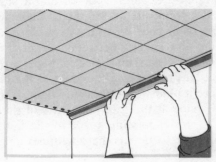

Molding to conceal nails.

Walls and Ceilings ● Chapter 6

7

Doors and Windows

S TICKING DOORS result from a number of factors—improper installation, excessive or insufficient atmospheric humidity, or house settling, to name but a few. Troublesome doors can usually be repaired easily by the handyperson with the right tools.

Jammed windows are essentially caused by the same problems and are likewise easily repaired. Repairing broken windows, when done carefully and methodically, is usually an even easier chore. The cost of replacing your broken windows may even be covered by your homeowner's insurance policy. Check with your agent to make sure, but such coverage is fairly standard. If you don't have such a provision in your contract, you might consider investing in this kind of protection. The cost is nominal and often pays for itself when the first pane breaks.

STICKING DOORS

A door swells when it is damp, and then becomes difficult to open and close. Before you attempt to plane off the door rails (top and bottom) or stiles (sides), it is wise to remember that the wood will shrink as the air dries out. Think twice before planing if you suspect that this is only a seasonal problem.

The first thing to check is the condition of the hinges. Position yourself on the side of the door opposite the stops (so that it closes away from you). With the door closed, examine the spaces between the door and frame. You can run a sheet of paper around the edges to observe the hang of the door; where it binds, the door is too tight. If there is a space at the top, latch side of the rail and a corresponding space at the bottom, hinge side, it means that the upper hinge is

probably loose, and perhaps the lower one as well.

Open the door to expose the hinges. Relieve pressure on the top hinge by having someone lightly support the door by its handle, or by slipping a wedge of some sort under the bottom rail. Use a broad-bladed screwdriver to tighten all the screws. If a screw does not appear to have any purchase, the wood around the screw has deteriorated. This can be corrected.

Remove the door by knocking out first the lower, then the upper hinge pin. Use a screwdriver angled so that the head of the pin is driven up and out. Should the pin be "frozen" or stuck, remove the hinge at the jamb. Inspect the mortise and the condition of the wood. If the holes look pulpy or rotted, hammer in a small wooden plug coated with glue or stuff the spaces with toothpicks or wooden matches dipped in glue, or fill them with plastic wood. Trim, then replace the hinge and rescrew, using longer screws if possible.

The difficulty may be that the hinge plate is not recessed deeply enough in the mortise, in which case you will have to chisel the mortise deeper. Or it may be possible, if spacing at the latch stile permits, to build up the lower hinge and thus shift the door to the vertical. The shim can be any piece of cardboard of the correct thickness (a matchbook cover serves well) and it should fill the mortise completely.

When the door binds along the entire length of the latch stile, you will have to cut the mortises deeper, as required. If necessary, you can deepen the mortises on both the jamb and the door.

Shimming will help if the door tends to spring open when you try to close it. In this case, place a strip of cardboard only behind half the width of the hinge leaf. You do not have to remove the hinge for this operation. Loosen the screws so that when the door is partially closed, the hinge leaf comes away from the mortise. Slip the shim into this space and tighten the screws. Shimming at this point serves to change the angle of the door so it leans toward the outside stop.

▲ If the hinge stile is catching or binding along the stop, you can reposition the hinge leaf in its mortise to pull the door away a bit, thus curing the problem.

FITTING A DOOR ▲

Often a door binds at several points at once because it or the frame has been warped out of shape. (Cracks or stress marks on the plaster around the frame are signs that the frame is at fault.) In either case, adjusting the fit of the hinges will not do the job completely. You will have to plane or sand the door as well.

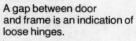
A gap between door and frame is an indication of loose hinges.

Support door while tightening screws.

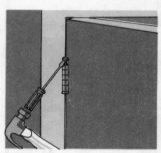
Knock out hinge pins.

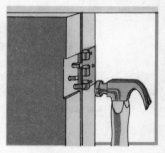
Fill screw holes.

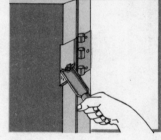
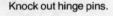
Deepen mortise.

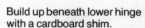
Insert shim behind half of hinge leaf.

Build up beneath lower hinge with a cardboard shim.

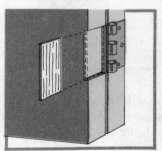

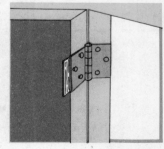

Plane sticking areas.

Shim behind striker plate.

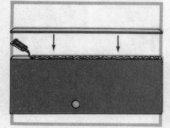

Build up door width.

Mortise for hinges.

Crayon on striker plate
locates problem area.

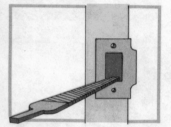

File striker plate receptacle.

Move plate, fill gaps.

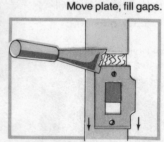

off the sticking areas while the door is closed, so that you will know how much has to be cut. Remove the door and prop it on its side against some solid support. Work the plane in smooth strokes, and do not bite too deeply at any one time. If the binding exists at the latch area of the door, it may prove simpler to plane the hinge side instead. Hinge leaves are easier to remove than the lock assembly.

When the door rubs at the top or bottom, you will have to plane one or both rails, either partially or fully. Keep in mind that you will be cutting across the grain, and if you work too roughly or use a dull tool it is easy to splinter the wood. If the amount to be removed is fractional, try a sanding block instead, but take care not to bevel the door edges.

A door sometimes becomes too narrow because of shrinkage, with the result that the latch is not able to reach the striker plate to engage it. If the distance is small, you can correct this by removing the striker plate and bringing it closer to the door with a wood or cardboard shim.

When the space to be filled is much wider, however, the best solution is to build up the width of the door by cementing and nailing a strip of wood along the hinge stile. The strip should be wide enough to close the gap and as thick as the stile. Measure to determine where the hinge leaves should be set, and chisel new mortises to receive them. The strip can be finished to match the finish on the door.

These adjustments to the door may create a problem: the door now swings freely but the latch is unable to engage the striker plate in the frame, with the result that the plate must be repositioned. To tell how much and in what direction, rub some crayon over the face of the striker plate and close the door. The resultant mark on the plate will indicate what has to be done.

If the latch is centered but falls short of

Your inspection will show where excess material has to be removed. Usually only a part of a side has to be touched up, rather than the entire length of a stile or rail. Mark

the receptacle in the plate, you might try filing the metal to bring the hole closer. Trim wood from the mortise, if required. If the entire plate has to be moved, fill the original screw holes with plugs before attempting to screw the plate in a new position. Gaps between the plate and the mortise can be filled with wood putty and touched up with paint. These same instructions apply when the plate must be moved up or down to meet the latch.

WINDOW PROBLEMS

When a wood window sash sticks or binds, it is usually because paint has worked into the sash molding or because the sash or frame has become swollen. Paint-stuck windows can sometimes be freed by tapping along both sides of the sash with a hammer and block of wood. If this does not free the window, insert the blade of a paint scraper or a broad, thin chisel between the sash and the stop molding. Tap the blade in with a hammer, then rock the tool back and forth gently to force the sash back from the molding. Repeat this at several points at each side of the sash until it can move freely. Never use a screwdriver for this job, as it will only gouge the wood.

If the sticking is severe, or if a seal forms at the bottom edge of the sash after a new paint job, the window can be pried loose from the outside without damage to the finish. A hatchet is a good tool for this, or any broad, hard metal wedge. Hammer the tool along the bottom of the sash, and pry as you go along. Once the window is free, scrape off any crusts of paint at the back face of the stop molding. Sand the molding lightly and touch up the window track.

If paint sticking is not the problem, it may be that the window has swollen permanently out of shape. Try the following

Tap gently along window to free it.

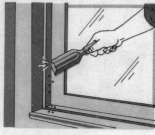
Insert chisel between sash and stop.

Pry from outside.

Scrape off paint, sand smooth.

method first: Cut a block of wood that will fit snugly into the channel between the inside and outside window stops above or below the sash. Give the block several smart raps with a hammer at both sides of the window. This should free the sash so that it can be raised (or lowered) at least partially. Repeat the procedure at the exposed channels at the bottom or top. A lubricant such as paraffin or candle wax may then be applied to the channels.

If this method fails, the sash will have to

Tap block in channel.

Repeat below raised window.

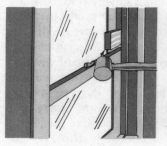

1. Remove window from tension strips.

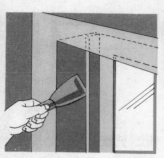

2. Remove stop molding on windows with sash cords.

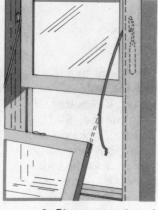

3. Disengage sash cord at both sides.

4. Keep sash from slipping past pulley.

5. Lubricate pulley.

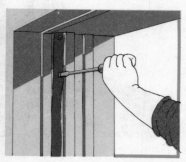

6. Adjust tension strips.

be removed from the frame to make the necessary adjustments. (In order to remove the top sash the bottom one must be taken out first.) Most modern windows are equipped with metal tension strips fastened to the channels. With this kind it may be possible to remove the sash simply by pressing it sideways into a channel and lifting it free.

On windows that have sash cords the stop molding must be removed first. Insert a broad chisel behind the molding and twist so that the strip comes away only partially at any one point. Work carefully to avoid damaging or breaking the molding. With the strip removed, disengage the sash cord at both sides. Fasten a nail or strip of wood to the ends of the cords so that they will not slip past the pulley. Lower the weight gently and observe the action of the pulley. If it is stiff, apply a few drops of oil to the pins.

If the window has tension strips, try ad-justing these first by turning their mounting screws. If this does not work, or if no mechanical adjustment is possible, wood can be sanded or planed from the sides of the sash to make it fit. Do not remove too much material at any one time. It is a good idea first to clean and lubricate the channels and then check the sash fit as you plane or sand. It should fit snugly without binding.

When a wood window rattles, it is because there is too much space between the sash and its stop molding. An easy way to alleviate this problem is to run a strip of metal or felt weatherstripping into the space. To make a permanent repair, remove the molding and nail it back closer to the sash.

Aluminum casement and sliding windows bind when dirt collects in the tracks. Sometimes the metal becomes pitted, impeding the window's smooth operation. Usually

Insert weatherstripping.

Renail molding.

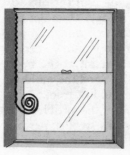

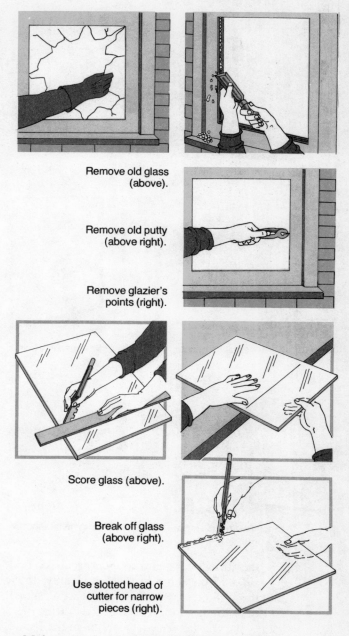

this can be corrected with a cleanup and rubbing with fine steel wool. The tracks should then be lubricated periodically with paraffin or wax. Never try to pry the window with a sharp tool, as this will distort the tracks.

When steel casement windows stick or bind, check to see that the hinges are free of rust or accumulated paint. Look for loose hinge screws or binding in the crank mechanism. Steel wool and lubricating oil will take care of the hinges. It may be necessary to open the handle assembly for cleaning and oiling.

INSTALLING GLASS

Replacing cracked or broken window glass is not difficult, but it requires some care. You will need a sharp glass cutter, prepared putty or glazing compound (more flexible than putty), and a putty knife.

Installation of the glass is normally done from the outside, so if you are repairing a second-floor window it is best to remove the sash, if that is possible. Wear heavy work gloves when removing the broken pieces of glass from the frame. Heat from a soldering gun will help soften the old putty, or a small wood chisel can be used to clean it out, but take care not to damage the frame. Extract the metal glazier's points with pliers.

The replacement glass should be cut 1/16 inch smaller all around than the frame opening. This is to allow for any irregularities that may exist in the frame.

Mark the glass with a sharpened crayon, then turn it over and lay it on a flat surface covered with a thickness of newspaper or an old blanket. A steel straightedge should be used to guide the cut. Any doubts about the glass cutter can be satisfied by first scoring a piece of the old glass; if the score mark shows signs of skipping, the cutting wheel is dull or chipped.

Remove old glass (above).

Remove old putty (above right).

Remove glazier's points (right).

Score glass (above).

Break off glass (above right).

Use slotted head of cutter for narrow pieces (right).

Make sure the glass is free of dust or grit before attempting the cut. The score mark should be begun just inside the edge of the glass farthest from you, then followed through with smooth, even pressure on the cutter. When the glass is scored, lay it over

Paint groove with linseed oil.

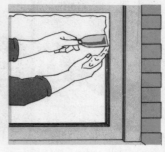

Apply bed of putty.

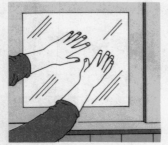

Press glass in place.

Insert glazier's points.

Smooth with putty knife.

Glazing metal windows.

the straightedge and apply pressure on both sides of the score to break it cleanly. If the piece to be removed is very narrow, snap it off with the slotted head of the cutting tool.

Before the glass is installed in the frame, the groove should be painted with linseed oil in order to prevent subsequent drying out and cracking of the putty. Apply a ⅛-inch thickness of putty all around the frame. Press the glass into place, making sure it lies flat against the shoulders of the frame. Secure it with the glazier's points, pressing them in 4 to 6 inches apart on all sides.

Now roll some more putty into a "rope" about ½ inch thick. Use your fingers to press it against the wood and glass around the frame. Smooth and bevel the compound with the blade of the putty knife, making sure that you leave no breaks or separations in the seal. A coat of paint neatly finishes the job.

For metal windows the procedure varies slightly. On these the glass panes are usually secured to the frames with small metal clips buried in the compound. These have to be removed and set aside.

Lay a bead of glazing compound into the metal frame and adjust the replacement glass so that the compound meets the glass at all sides. Install the clips, then apply the final bead of compound. If there are metal strips, screw them back in place.

In numerous instances people have seriously injured themselves by walking into or putting their hands through large windows or doors. Safety and consumer agencies have been urging legislation requiring the use of less hazardous materials in such vulnerable places as sliding patio doors, storm doors, shower doors, tub enclosures, and other areas where standard glass might constitute a hazard.

Laws incorporating these recommendations have already been passed by several states. These require that "safety glazing material" be used in potentially dangerous areas such as those mentioned above. Some of the safety materials are tempered glass, laminated glass, wire glass, and acrylic plastic.

These materials may be slightly more difficult to install than regular glass, and their cost is generally higher. By installing these materials in place of standard glass panes, however, the extra cost is offset by the sense of security in knowing one's house is safe. One thing to watch out for with the rigid plastic materials such as acrylics, though, is surface mars. Whereas their lesser hardness makes them less susceptible to breakage than glass, it also increases their chances of being nicked or scratched.

SCREEN REPAIR

Keep your window and door screens in good condition by stacking them flat in a dry, well-ventilated area until ready for use. Wood frames should be tightened when necessary and given a fresh coat of paint from time to time to help preserve them.

A small hole in screening has a mysterious way of increasing in size if not patched as soon as it is discovered. If the hole is small enough, a drop or two of waterproof cement will do the job. The cement hardens into a film that covers the hole.

When dealing with larger tears, cut a patch of wire screen material that is wider than the hole by ½-inch. If you do not have extra screening around, patches in various sizes are available at any hardware store.

Unravel two wires at each side of the patch, then bend the end wires at a right angle on all four sides. Place the patch over the hole and thread the bent wires so that they pass evenly to the other side of the screen. They can now be bent back to fix the patch permanently and firmly.

An old or damaged wood screen frame can be renewed easily enough so that you do not have to go to the expense of purchasing a new one. When trouble occurs, it is usually at the frame joints.

A joint can be tightened by bracing the frame pieces with a ⅜-inch dowel. Drill a hole through the side member into the top or bottom piece. Coat the dowel with glue and hammer it into the hole, trimming or driving it flush, as the case may be.

A sagging screen door can be corrected with the use of a turnbuckle and cable, placed from one side of the door to the other. Fasten one end of the cable to the top side rail over the hinge; the other end should be screwed to the bottom of the other side rail. Tighten the turnbuckle until the door can swing freely.

Patch a small hole in the screen with cement (left).

Place a patch over the hole if it is bigger (below left).

Fold ends under to seal permanently (below).

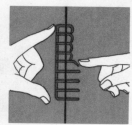

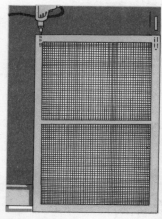

Doweling a corner joint (above).

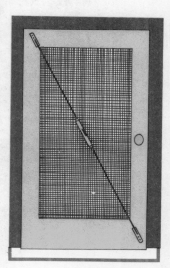

Repair for a sagging screen door using a turnbuckle and cable (right).

To replace screen wire in a wood frame, you must first remove the molding. Use a paint scraper or putty knife for this job, prying gently along the length of the molding until it comes free. Remove all staples or tacks from the frame. Cut the new screen 1 inch wider on all sides with old scissors or metal snips.

Tension must be applied to the screen when it is tacked to the frame, in order to prevent any stretching later. The best way to do this is to lay the frame across a work surface as wide as the frame (two boards across a pair of sawhorses make a good work surface). Place a board under each end of the frame, then C-clamp the sides of the frame to the work surface so that there is a slight bow formed in the middle.

Tack the new screening tautly at each end, doubling the material where you tack. Now release the C-clamps and tack the screen along the sides of the frame. Replace the molding and trim any wire that sticks out from under it.

In metal frames, a spline holds the screening in place. This must be pried out to remove the torn screening. New screening is then laid over the framing and trimmed to size, with the corners cut at 45-degree angles. The spline is then tapped back into its groove in the frame to secure the screening.

Remove screen molding.

Remove staples, tacks.

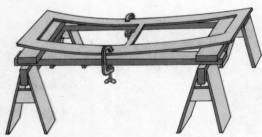

Set up screen for repair.

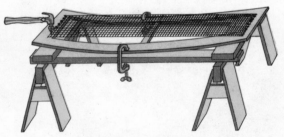

Tack new screening at each end.

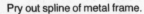

Pry out spline of metal frame.

Tap spline into groove.

Trim screening.

8

Weatherproofing and Insulating

YOUR HOUSE should be adequately ventilated even in winter, but this does not mean that unregulated drafts of cold air should be allowed to sweep through the house. In cold weather, warm air escapes around loose windows and doors and is replaced by cold outdoor air. Outdoor windiness tends to increase heat loss considerably. The result is that the output of the heating plant has to be increased to maintain the desired house temperature, and on cold windy days, if such leaks are extreme, it may be difficult to keep the house warm. In hot weather, it is just as important to keep out the heat and keep in the cool.

WEATHERSTRIPPING

Weatherstripping of doors and windows is one method of increasing comfort and reducing the consumption of fuel, whether oil or gas for heating or electricity for summer air conditioning.

Many kinds and grades of weatherstripping are available at various prices. They include metal and wood in rigid form and fabric (usually felt), rubber, and vinyl in rigid and flexible form.

The rigid types are made of strips of wood or metal to which are fastened flexible rubber strips or sponge backing. An interlocking rigid metal type is available, but use of this should be left to the professional, since it involves the removal of sash and cutting of precise grooves.

The flexible types are the best choice for the do-it-yourselfer. The felt types are the least expensive, shortest-lived of the lot. Vinyl stripping is more attractive, more ex-

pensive, and wears longer. Adhesive-backed foam rubber does not last a long time, but it may be your only choice for metal windows to which you cannot nail the material. The spring metal stripping is the most expensive, but it is also permanent.

For the bottoms of doors, special rigid weatherstripping is available. The simplest

Types of flexible weatherstripping.

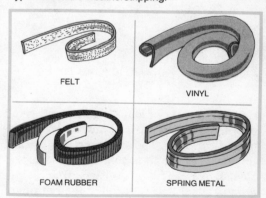

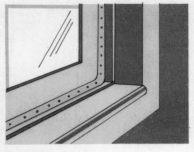

Installation of
flexible weatherstripping.

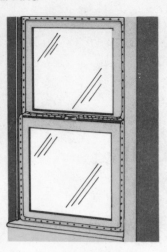

Installation of flexible
weatherstripping
on double-hung window.

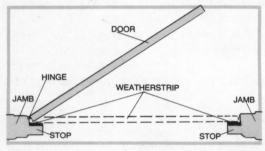

Installatiion on a door.

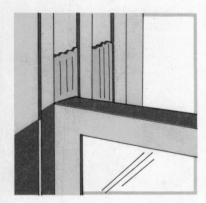

Spring-type installation
on window.

type is a metal or aluminum strip with a felt or vinyl sweep that is screwed to the bottom of the door. The sweep presses against the inside of the threshold when the door is closed. Another type consists of an aluminum channel that fits around the bottom of the door like a sleeve. It has a flexible vinyl facing that presses down over the top of the threshold. Yet another kind replaces the threshold entirely, and has a vinyl inset that provides a seal against the door bottom.

Flexible weatherstripping is easy to install. Most types can be cut with scissors; tin snips are needed for others. It should be fastened so that the flexible, or contact, edge presses snugly against a face of the closed window or door. Bend the stripping at corners to form a continuous seal, where possible. It should be screwed or nailed every 3 or 4 inches and at every corner.

On double-hung windows the weatherstripping should be applied in three pieces, one for each sash and a shorter length to fit where the two sashes meet. Install the sash sections in one continuous strip, nailing the sides to the window stops· and the upper and lower sections to the sill and frame. Tack the shorter piece along the top of the lower sash so that it presses against the upper sash. It may be necessary to cut the stripping to fit around the sash lock.

On doors the weatherstripping is fastened in one piece around the door stops. Its placement on the stops depends on the type of stripping used. The felt and foam types are applied to the inside face of the stops. Vinyl tubular stripping should be tacked to the side of the stop so that it presses evenly against the face of the door.

Casement windows are sealed in a similar fashion, with the stripping fastened to the stops. Channel stripping of either metal or vinyl should be used for steel windows.

Spring bronze or aluminum stripping is cut into lengths and placed on the inside of a window channel and at the jambs and frame of a door. It is of two-ply construction, one leaf of which is tacked to the wood while the other presses out against the sides of a window or door to form a draft-resisting seal.

To install on a window, raise the sash and

nail the strips to the sash channels with the open leaf facing the outside. Each strip should be long enough so that an inch or so of spring is still tucked under the sash when the sash is full up or down. This permits the window to be closed without having to depress the spring. A small section of spring should be tacked along the bottom face of the upper sash.

On doors, fasten the spring in three sections to the jambs and frame just inside the stops; again, the spring leaf should be facing the outside.

INSULATION IN ATTICS

Insulation in ceilings and walls is vital for keeping your home comfortable year-round. Two basic kinds of insulation are available for floors of unheated attics. Both will do the job if they are properly installed. One type is preformed mineral fiber (glass fiber or rock wool) batts or blankets. The other type is cellulose or mineral fiber in loose-fill form.

When installing insulation in attics, you don't have to stop at the ceiling joists if the attic has no flooring, but insulation should not touch the roof at the eaves. If you have a finished attic, check with an insulation specialist for the proper procedure for installing insulation.

Preformed insulation batts may be more economical than loose-fill materials in an unobstructed attic area without flooring, if they fit snugly between the joists and you do the work yourself. You can add insulation to your attic in one afternoon using batts—they can be laid out easily and there is no need to staple them down.

Once the area between the joists is fully insulated, the greatest source of heat loss in the attic is through the joists themselves, which may cover as much as 10 percent of the attic. For this reason, when adding insulation batts above the level of the ceiling joists, cover joists completely if possible.

▲ Loose-fill insulation may be better if the access to your attic is difficult or if it has a floor. If flooring is present in an otherwise unfinished attic, you may have to remove some of it temporarily to allow insulation to be blown in. Loose insulation is usually blown into the attic through flexible tubing by a small machine that puffs up the insulation as it pushes it through the tube. You may be able to rent such a machine at a large rental store. There may be some settling after the insulation is in place, so you should take that into account when measuring the depth.

The density of loose-fill insulation is extremely important in assuring the proper resistance to heat flow. The manufacturer generally specifies the number of bags of loose-fill materials needed for a specific area. If a contractor is insulating your attic, you should verify that the proper number of bags has been used.

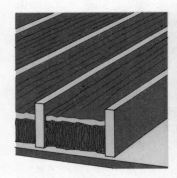 

Fitting preformed insulation batts between joists (above).

Cover joists completely with insulation batts (above right).

Removing flooring to install loose-fill insulation (right).

A well-insulated attic should also be well ventilated to prevent moisture accumulation. Never block ventilation ports, and always provide at least two vent openings located in such a way that air can flow in one and out the other. A good rule of thumb is to provide at least one square foot of opening for each 300 square feet of attic floor.

When inspecting your attic, you may notice interior wall spaces open to the attic, allowing cold air from the attic to fall down into the wall spaces or duct wells. These areas should be covered with insulation.

INSULATION IN EXTERIOR WALLS

● About 3 or 4 inches of insulation properly placed in the wall cavity can reduce the heat transfer through walls by as much as two-thirds. The best time to install insulation in this wall space is when the house is being built. When the wall is open, it is most economical to fill the wall space with batt insulation. Unfinished garage walls next to heated areas of the house should be insulated with batts.

▪ Once a wall is finished off, it is difficult to reach the air space, and insulation has to be blown or injected into the wall through small holes drilled between the wall studs. (This can be done from the outside or the inside, depending on the ease of sealing the holes and refinishing the surface.) Loose-fill materials, usually mineral fiber or cellulose, are the insulation forms best suited for this job. Although this process is much more costly than adding batt insulation during construction, it may still be a good investment if done properly. Only an experienced contractor should be employed, however, as the process can be quite complicated and poor workmanship will greatly lower the quality of the finished work.

Loose-fill wall insulation is recommended only for exterior walls with an air space at least 3 to 4 inches wide and with no existing insulation.

▲ In some older houses, access can be gained to the wall space from the attic. In this case, loose-fill insulation material can be dropped into the space from above at very low cost, making this economical in all but the mildest climates with low fuel prices. Just make sure the insulation doesn't fall all the way into the basement!

A potential problem with insulation in closed cavities in some climates is the possibility of moisture accumulation. This may be difficult to detect until moisture begins to show through the wall. If moisture problems occur, they can be minimized. The interior surface of the wall can be made vapor-resistant with a paint or covering that has low-moisture permeability. Cracks around windows and door frames, electrical outlets, and baseboards should be sealed at the surface facing the room. Outside surfaces should not be tightly sealed but allowed to "breathe."

Another potential problem that you may encounter with blown-in insulation is settling or shrinkage. Generally, this can be avoided if the insulation is properly installed. Calculating the number of bags of material needed per square foot of wall area and assuring that the full quantity has been installed is the best way to avoid this problem.

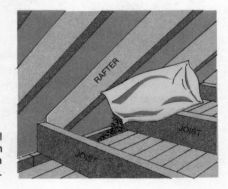

Installing wall insulation in older construction from attic.

RAFTER

JOIST

JOIST

9

Condensation Problems

CONDENSATION is the change in moisture from a vapor to a liquid. In homes not properly protected, condensation caused by high humidity often results in excessive maintenance costs. Water vapor within the house, when unrestricted, can move through the wall or ceiling during the heating season to some cold surface where it condenses, collecting generally in the form of ice or frost. During warm periods the frost melts. When conditions are severe, the water from melting ice in unvented attics may drip to the ceiling below and cause damage to the interior finish. Moisture can also soak into the roof sheathing or rafters and set up conditions that could lead to decay. In walls, water from melting frost may run out between the siding laps and cause staining, or it may soak into the siding and cause paint blistering and peeling.

WHEN DOES IT OCCUR AND WHERE?

Wood and wood-base materials used for sheathing and panel siding may swell from this added moisture and result in bowing, cupping, or buckling. Thermal insulation also becomes wet and provides less resistance to heat loss.

The cost of heat loss, painting and redecorating, and excessive maintenance and repair caused by cold-weather condensation can easily be reduced or eliminated by proper construction details.

Estimates have been made that a typical family of four converts 3 gallons of water into water vapor per day. Unless excess water vapor is properly removed in some way (ventilation usually), it will either in-

crease the humidity or condense on cold surfaces such as window glass. More serious, however, it can move in or through the construction, often condensing within the wall, roof, or floor cavities. Heating systems equipped with winter air-conditioning systems also increase the humidity.

Most new houses have from 2 to 3½ inches of insulation in the walls and 6 or more inches in the ceilings. Unfortunately, the more efficient the insulation is in retarding heat transfer, the colder the outer surfaces become and, unless moisture is restricted from entering the wall or ceiling, the greater the potential for moisture condensation. Moisture migrates toward cold surfaces and condenses or forms as frost or ice on these surfaces.

Inexpensive methods of preventing condensation problems are available. They mainly involve the proper use of vapor barriers and good ventilating practices. Naturally it is simpler, less expensive, and more effective to employ these during the construction of a house than to add them to existing homes.

Condensation takes place any time the temperature drops below the dew point (100 percent saturation of the air with water vapor at a given temperature). Commonly, under such conditions some surface accessible to the moisture in the air is cooler than the dew point, and the moisture condenses on that surface.

During cold weather, visible condensation is usually first noticed on window glass, but it may also be discovered on cold surfaces of closet and unheated bedroom walls and ceilings. Condensation may also be visible in attic spaces on rafters or roof boards near the cold cornice area, or it might form as frost. Such condensation or melting frost can result in excessive maintenance costs, such as the need for refinishing of window sash and trim, or even decay. Water from melting frost in the attic can also damage ceilings below.

Another area in which visible condensation can occur is in crawl spaces under occupied rooms. This area usually differs from those in the interior of the house and in the attic because the source of the moisture is usually from the soil or from warm moisture-laden air that enters through foundation ventilators. Moisture vapor then condenses on the cooler surfaces in the crawl space. Such conditions often occur during warm periods in late spring.

An increase in the relative humidity of the inside atmosphere increases the potential for condensation on inside surfaces. For example, when the inside temperature is 70 degrees F, surface condensation will occur on a single-thickness glass window when the outside temperature falls to -10 degrees F and the inside relative humidity is 10 percent. When the inside relative humidity is 20 percent, condensation can occur on the single glass when the outside temperature falls only to about +7 degrees F. When a storm window is added or insulated glass is used, surface condensation does not occur until the relative humidity has reached 38 percent when the outdoor temperature is -10 degrees F. These conditions apply only if storm windows are tight and there is good circulation of air on the inside surface of the window. If draperies or shades restrict circulation of air, storm windows are not tight, or lower temperatures are maintained in such areas as bedrooms, condensation occurs at a higher outside temperature.

Condensation in concealed areas, such as wall cavities, often is first revealed by stains on the siding or by paint peeling. Water vapor moving through permeable walls and ceilings is normally responsible for such damage. Water vapor also escapes from houses by constant outleakage through cracks and crevices, around doors and windows, and by ventilation, but this moisture-vapor loss is usually insufficient to eliminate condensation problems.

MOISTURE SOURCES

Moisture that is produced in or enters a home changes the relative humidity of the interior atmosphere. Ordinary household functions that generate a good share of the total amount of water vapor include dishwashing, cooking, bathing, and laundry work; add to this human respiration and evaporation from plants. Houses may also be equipped with central winter air conditioners or room humidifiers. Still another source of moisture may be from unvented or poorly vented clothes dryers.

Condensation problems can best be eliminated by specifying proper construction

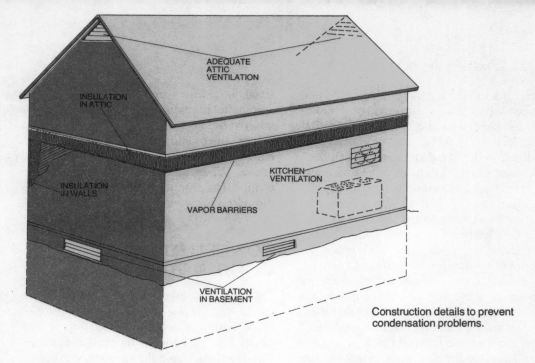

Construction details to prevent condensation problems.

details during planning of the house. Correct placement of vapor barriers, adequate insulation, the use of attic ventilation, and other good practices can be incorporated at this time. When these details have not been included in an existing house and condensation problems occur, they are often more difficult to solve. Nevertheless, there are methods to minimize such problems after the house has been built.

VISIBLE CONDENSATION

● Visible condensation on the interior glass surfaces of windows can be minimized by the use of storm windows or by replacing single-thickness glass with insulated glass. When this does not prevent condensation, however, the relative humidity in the room must be reduced. Draperies or curtains across the windows hinder rather than help. Not only do they increase surface condensation by keeping the glass surfaces colder, but they also prevent the air movement that would warm the glass surface and aid in dispersing some of the moisture.

▲ Condensation or frost on protruding nails, on the surfaces of roof boards, or other structural members in attic areas normally indicates the escape of excessive amounts of water vapor from the heated rooms below. If a vapor barrier is not already present, place one between joists under the insulation. Make sure the vapor

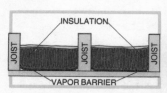

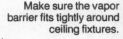

Vapor barrier between attic joists.

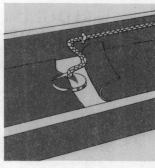

Make sure the vapor barrier fits tightly around ceiling fixtures.

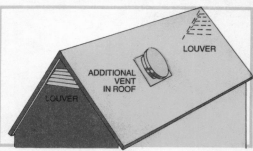

Add ventilators in attic.

barrier fits tightly around ceiling lights and exhaust fans, calking if necessary. In addition, increase both inlet and outlet ventilators. Decreasing the amount of water vapor produced in the living areas is also helpful.

▲ Surface condensation in unheated crawl spaces is usually caused by excessive moisture from the soil or from warm, humid air entering from outside the house. To eliminate this problem, place a vapor barrier over the soil; if necessary, increase the amount of ventilation (see CHAPTER 10).

● Concrete slabs without radiant heat are sometimes subjected to surface condensation in late spring when warm humid air enters the house. Because the temperature of some areas of the concrete slab or its covering is below the dew point, surface condensation can occur. Keeping the windows closed during the day, using a dehumidifier, and raising the inside temperature aid in minimizing this problem. When the concrete slab reaches normal room temperature, this inconvenience is eliminated.

REDUCING RELATIVE HUMIDITY

Reducing high relative humidities within the house to permissible levels is often necessary to minimize condensation problems. It is helpful to discontinue the use of room-sized humidifiers or reduce the output of automatic humidifiers until conditions are improved. The use of exhaust fans and dehumidifiers can also be of value in eliminating high relative humidities within the house. When possible, decreasing the activities that produce excessive moisture, as discussed previously, is sometimes helpful.

CONCEALED CONDENSATION

Concealed condensation is essentially a surface or similar condensation that takes place within a component such as a wall cavity when a condensing surface is below the dew point. In cold weather, condensation often forms as frost. Such conditions can cause staining of siding and peeling of the paint and possibly decay in severe and sustained conditions. These problems are usually not detected until spring, after the heating season has ended. The remedies should be taken care of before repainting or re-siding is attempted. Several methods may be used to correct these problems: reduce or control the relative humidity within the house; add a vapor-resistant paint coating such as aluminum paint to the interior of walls and ceilings; improve the vapor resistance of the ceiling joists; and improve attic ventilation.

10

Basements, Crawl Spaces

A LARGE PORTION of your home's usable space—as much as 50 percent in some ranch houses—is in the basement. Finished off, it becomes a family room, sewing room, den, office, or extra bedrooms. Unfortunately, many basements have dampness problems that must be cleared up before that space can be utilized.

Even if the basement is not to be finished off, such problems should be cured. Basement dampness affects comfort in the rooms overhead. It makes basement storage undesirable or impossible. And the dampness may be a warning of more serious troubles to come if it is not checked. Such a condition should never be ignored. But before corrective action can be taken, the cause of the problem must be pinpointed.

WHAT'S YOUR PROBLEM?

Almost all basement dampness problems can be traced to one of three causes: leakage, seepage, or condensation.

Leakage is usually obvious, occurring during a heavy rainfall or when snow is melting. An excessive amount of water builds up in the soil around the foundation walls, forcing its way through cracks or other defects in poured concrete walls (such as small holes around form wires), or through poor mortar joints in a concrete-block wall. If the area around the foundation has been improperly backfilled or graded, the situation is aggravated. In very wet periods, considerable flooding may result.

Seepage is evidenced by large areas of dampness on the foundation walls, rather than by water leaking through a particular spot. Usually, it will be greatest along the lower parts of the wall. Like leakage, it is caused by excessive water pressure on the outside of the basement walls. It may also be due to capillary action, which draws water from the moist soil through porous sections of the masonry.

Leakage in poured concrete (above) and concrete block walls (above right).

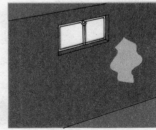

Seepage or condensation (right).

Test indicating condensation.

Test indicating seepage.

indicating that condensation is to blame. If the surface of the patch is dry and clear while the surrounding wall is damp, seepage is the problem.

CONDENSATION CURES

If condensation is the cause of your moisture miseries, the remedy is to dry out the air in the basement as much as possible.

Adequate ventilation is essential for a dry basement. In cool, dry weather, keep the basement windows open whenever possible. On hot, humid days, keep them closed; warm, moist air may even cause mildew to form on the cooler masonry walls. If your basement has too few windows to provide needed ventilation, a small exhaust fan installed in a window or ducted to the outside will help.

Pipes that tend to sweat in hot weather should be wrapped with insulation. This is especially important if finishing off the basement ceiling is part of your plans. Otherwise, moisture dripping from the pipes will ruin your ceiling tiles or panels.

Clothes dryers should always be vented to the outside. This is a relatively easy do-it-yourself job. The vent pipe is normally run through a hole in the header joist or stringer joist (these are the joists that rest on the sills, which in turn are bolted to the top of the foundation walls). The hole can be cut either from inside the basement or, with careful measurements, from outside. Its diameter will depend on the size of the

Condensation looks very much like seepage, but here the moisture comes from air inside the basement, not from water outside (although seepage from outside may be a factor in creating the conditions for condensation). Condensation usually occurs during warm, humid weather, when the cool masonry walls seem to "sweat." It can also happen during colder months when warm air is discharged by a clothes dryer or similar appliance; moisture from this air collects on the cooler walls in the form of droplets, which may be mistaken for seepage from outside.

There is a simple test to determine whether a damp wall is the result of seepage or condensation. Tape a small mirror or a piece of sheet metal to the wall (or use a waterproof mastic if it is too wet for tape to stick). Leave it there overnight and inspect it the next day. If the surface of the mirror is fogged or the sheet metal damp, the moisture came from inside the basement,

1. Cut hole for vent of clothes dryer.

2. Insert hooded fitting through the hole.

3. Attach flexible pipe to the fitting of dryer's exhaust port.

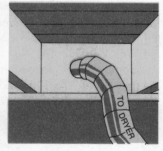

Chapter 10 • Basements, Crawl Spaces

exhaust port on your dryer. Use a saber saw or keyhole saw to cut the hole, after first drilling a ½-inch or larger pilot hole. Insert a hooded fitting through the hole from the outside, then connect the dryer's exhaust port to this fitting with flexible pipe. Both the fitting and flexible pipe can be purchased at most hardware stores.

If you do not have a clothes dryer, try to avoid hanging clothes to dry in the basement. The moisture from the wet clothes will enter the air and show up as condensation on the walls.

When basement condensation persists, an electric dehumidifier or chemical drying agents may be needed to remove moisture from the air and keep the basement dry.

CONDENSATION IN NEW HOUSES

If you are one of the fortunate few who have been able to move into brand-new houses in this time of skyrocketing costs and astronomical-interest mortgages, chances are that your condensation problems are greater than most. Condensation is at its maximum in new houses. During construction, literally tons of water are used—in concrete, mortar, plaster, wallpaper paste, tile work, and even many types of paint. This water gradually evaporates, giving a higher moisture content than normal to the air throughout the house and ending up as condensation on basement walls and windows in every room.

All the steps described above (especially providing adequate ventilation) should be employed to assist this normal drying-out process. In addition, be patient. Do not try to accelerate the process by turning up the furnace to extremely high temperatures. This will only cause uneven drying, exaggerating the effects of normal materials shrinkage and almost surely resulting in greater patch-and-repair problems later on.

SEEPAGE SOLUTIONS

If seepage is the cause of your basement dampness, a simple coat of paint may be the solution. Not just any paint, of course, but one that is resistant to water, alkali, and mildew and has good adhesion to concrete. This will provide a watertight coating that is durable and decorative.

Most such paints can be applied to both damp and uncured concrete as well as to previously painted surfaces. As with any paint job, the key to success is careful preparation.

Unpainted concrete, new or old, must be clean before application of paint. Grease, oil, and dirt should be removed with a strong cleansing agent such as trisodium phosphate. After scrubbing with a stiff-bristled brush, rinse the surface thoroughly with water to remove all residue. Allow to dry for 24 hours.

On a previously painted wall, all paint that is flaking, blistering, cracking, or chalking must be removed. This is done by scraping and brushing with a wire brush. Chemical removers can also be used. As with new concrete, the surface should then be scrubbed clean, rinsed, and allowed to dry thoroughly.

If the walls are whitewashed, scrub them with a dilute mixture of muriatic acid (10 parts water to 1 part acid). Wear rubber gloves and protective glasses or goggles for this job, and be careful not to splash any of the mixture on your skin or in your eyes. If you do, wash it off immediately with plenty of water. Again, rinse the surface thoroughly after scrubbing, and allow it to dry.

Before painting, patch large cracks and holes in the concrete, following the directions given below for plugging leaks. Hairline cracks and pores or pinholes need not be filled; the full-bodied paint will cover them.

Apply the paint with a brush or roller,

covering the surface evenly and thoroughly. Normally, a single coat does the job, but if the concrete or concrete block is very porous a second coat may be required.

■ A more serious seepage problem suggests a structural fault that will probably have to be corrected from outside the wall. You may prefer to leave this project to the professionals, since it involves excavating a trench wide enough to allow working space and deep enough to reach the problem area. The masonry surface must then be scrubbed clean before a coating of cement plaster is troweled on. This is followed by a second coating and, finally, a coating of asphalt cement or plastic sealer.

▲ Where subsoil moisture is present in excessive amounts, causing the seepage problem, drain tile should be laid around the foundation footings to carry water away from the house—another digging project. Tiles should be pitched downward ¼ inch per foot toward the drainage point. Joints between tiles should be covered with strips of tar paper to keep out dirt, and the tiles should both rest on and be covered by a layer of gravel or crushed stone.

STOPPING LEAKS

● When water is trickling through the basement wall, your first step is to plug the leak. This is best done with a quick-setting hydraulic cement that can be applied even when a crack is under pressure—that is, when water is pouring through it. Apply the cement with a trowel or wide-blade putty knife, holding it in place until the flow of water is stopped.

Such patches are usually only temporary and should be replaced when the crack is dry. For a normal dry repair, first chisel out the crack to form an inverted V-groove, about ½ inch at the surface and wider beneath so that the patching material will be locked in place. Use a cold chisel and a 1-pound ball pein or mash hammer for this job (your claw hammer should be reserved for carpentry and woodworking projects). Clean away all loose rubble and dust, and wire-brush clean. Flush with water to remove all dust particles.

Mix together 1 part cement to 2½ parts of clean sand. Add enough water to make a stiff mixture, making sure to wet all parts of

Plugging the leak with cement.

Chiseling crack.

Fill crack with patching cement.

Scrape defective mortar joint.

Force mortar into joint.

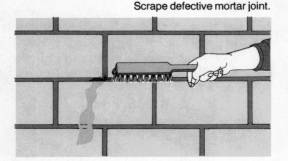

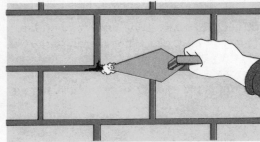

the sand-cement. Dampen the area to be patched, then force the mixture into the crack with a trowel, filling it completely. Keep the patched area slightly damp for a few days to allow the cement to cure thoroughly. If that doesn't solve your leakage problem, you will probably have to attack it from outside, as described for seepage.

In a concrete-block foundation wall, water may leak through a defective mortar joint between blocks. To repair this, first scrape away all loose and crumbling mortar, using a cold chisel or an old screwdriver. Clean out the joint with a wire brush and rinse with water to remove all dust particles. Make a mortar mix of 1 part masonry cement to 3 parts clean, dry sand. Add enough water to make a workable but fairly stiff mixture. Force the mortar into the joint with a trowel, striking it off flush with the surface of the block. Allow the mortar to dry thoroughly.

▲ Leaks at the wall-floor joint can similarly be corrected with cement. Even more effective is a two-part epoxy resin compound that forms a durable seal against hydrostatic pressure at this point. Once again, the area should be thoroughly cleaned before making the repair. The material is mixed immediately before use and brushed or troweled into place. Two coats are usually recommended.

▲ Leaks in concrete floors are repaired in the same way as wall leaks: undercutting, cleaning, and patching with a sand-cement mixture. However, floor leaks may be indicative of more serious problems. Your home may be in a very low, wet location or be built over a marshy area or an underground stream. In that case, a drainage tile system may have to be installed, as described above for major seepage problems.

CRAWL SPACES

Crawl spaces present some special problems because cold and dampness commonly invade these areas. Occasionally, unpleasant odors result. These conditions make living on the floor above somewhat less than ideal. The conditions are usually curable.

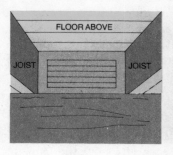
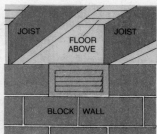
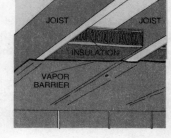

Install vent in leader joist (above).

Install vent in block wall (above right).

Insulation to prevent cold floors over crawl spaces (right).

Again, adequate ventilation is essential. There should be vents or louvers on at least two opposite sides of the crawl space to provide cross-ventilation. If necessary, you can install vents by cutting holes through the header joists (similar to installing a dryer vent, described above). If the foundation is of concrete block, you can simply knock out a block to emplace a vent. Louvered vents, which can be closed off in damp or cold weather, are best. Most of them are also screened to keep out rodents and other small animals.

Cold floors in rooms over crawl spaces present another problem. The best solution is to install 4-inch insulation batts between the floor joists. Staple the batts to the bottoms of the joists, forming air space between the subfloor and the insulation. (Don't block vents with the insulation.) Below the insulation, staple a vapor barrier of heavy felt paper. This will seal out any moisture. Make sure that the entire area beneath the floor is covered.

If dampness persists, cover the ground in the crawl space with tar paper. Overlap the joints 3 to 4 inches, and seal the tar paper to the foundation walls with asphalt compound. Then spread a 2-inch layer of dry sand over the tar paper. This should insure that the area above the crawl space will be cozy and dry the year round.

PREVENTIVE MEASURES

Patching holes and cracks and waterproofing basement walls solve the immediate problems of leakage and seepage, but since the ultimate cause is excess water accumulation in the ground around the foundation walls, this situation should also be corrected. This is done by making provision to divert surface water before it can come into contact with the foundation.

Check gutters and downspouts for leaks or improper pitching that may cause water to collect along the foundation wall. Gutters that are clogged with leaves and other debris may also divert water onto the ground beside the house and, eventually, into the basement. Downspouts should be connected to a storm sewer or to an underground dry well located at least 10 feet away from the foundation. Downspouts not so connected should empty onto concrete splash blocks that carry the water runoff away from the house walls.

To carry away rainwater as quickly as possible, the ground surface should slope away sharply at foundation walls, then more gradually to at least 10 feet from the walls. If such is not the case, fill in with new soil, taking special care in areas where puddles form during rainy weather. Tamp the soil firmly and sow it with good grass seed or sod rolled down evenly and firmly. If the new grading extends above basement windows, protect each one with a curved

metal shell or concrete wall. Gravel in the bottoms of these protected areas will facilitate drainage. Hinged plastic covers may be provided to admit light but keep out rain and snow.

Where concrete walks or driveways are adjacent to the foundation wall, they should also slope away gradually. The walk-wall joint should be concave or sharply angled to keep out water. If the joints are not so protected, or if they are broken or otherwise damaged, they should be fixed.

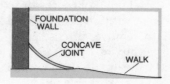

Walk-wall joint.

Chip away loose or damaged concrete. Scrub clean both the wall and the walk, and roughen both surfaces with a cold chisel and peining hammer. You can then apply an epoxy resin compound to the joint, as described above for basement wall-floor joints. Or you can use a mixture of 1 part cement to 2½ parts sand. Moisten the concrete surfaces, then trowel the cement-sand mixture into the joint, sloping it sharply away from the foundation wall for a minimum of 2 inches.

A FINAL NOTE OF CAUTION

If all else fails and you must call in a professional to try to solve your basement dampness problem, exercise a degree of caution and beware of "miracle cures." There are many highly reputable firms in the basement waterproofing business, but there are also some of lesser repute. Follow the usual practice of checking with the local Better Business Bureau, consumer protection groups, and other homeowners who have dealt with the firm before you sign any contract. As ever, let the buyer beware.

Chapter 10 • Basements, Crawl Spaces

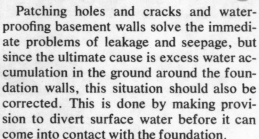

Downspouts should carry water away from foundation.

CONCRETE SPLASH BLOCK

11

Controlling Household Pests

SOME HOUSEHOLD pests have an incredible ability to escape extinction. Cockroaches, for example, which have been on the earth millions of years longer than man, can subsist on any kind of food; they thrive in all parts of the world. Some species of cockroaches prefer man's home to other habitats. Once they enter it, they use countless instinctive tricks to keep from being evicted.

You can help control household pests by systematic housecleaning. You can rid your home of practically all pests, and keep it free of them, by a combination of continuous good housekeeping and the proper use of the right pesticide at the right time.

PESTICIDES AND THEIR APPLICATION

Pesticides may be applied in different forms and different ways to serve various purposes. Surface sprays are applied to surfaces in the home where insects are likely to crawl. The spray particles are coarse, and they dampen or wet the surfaces. When the spray dries, a thin deposit of insecticide remains. For several weeks or months, the deposit kills insects that crawl over it.

You may buy these sprays in pressurized containers, or you may buy a liquid insecticide and apply it with a household hand sprayer that produces a coarse spray.

Do not spray oil-base insecticides on asphalt-tile floors, because they may dissolve the asphalt. They may also soften and discolor some linoleums and some plastic materials; if in doubt about spraying such surfaces, test the spray on a small, inconspicuous place. If you apply an oil-base insecticide to the cracks in a parquet floor, apply it lightly; an excessive amount may dissolve the underlying cement, and the dissolved cement may stain the floor.

Space sprays and aerosols are designed for application into the air. They are especially effective against mosquitoes, houseflies, and other flying insects. They may also be used to penetrate the hiding places of other insects such as roaches, driving them into the open where they may be killed with a surface spray or dust.

The particles, or droplets, of a space spray are much finer than those of a surface spray, and float in the air for a time. The particles of an aerosol are fine than those of a space spray, and float in the air for a longer time.

Space sprays leave little residue, and generally should not be used as surface sprays. Aerosols are entirely too fine for surface application.

You may buy space sprays in pressurized containers; or you may buy liquid insecti-

HAND SPRAYER

cide and apply it as a space spray with a household hand sprayer having a nozzle that produces very fine particles. Household aerosols are available in pressurized containers.

Some sprays sold in pressurized containers may be labeled for both surface and space applications. If you use one of these products for spraying in the kitchen or pantry, first place cooking and eating utensils, and food, where they will not be contaminated by falling particles.

Before applying a space spray or aerosol, close all windows and doors tightly. Apply the chemical into the air as directed on the container label. Some people may be allergic to the materials in space sprays or aerosols. After application, it is advisable to leave the room, close the door, and not reenter for half an hour or longer. Breathe as little as possible of the chemicals discharged in space sprays or aerosols.

Insecticidal dusts usually contain the same active ingredients as sprays. They are used for surface applications, and may be blown by a household hand duster into cracks, corners, and other places difficult to reach with sprays.

HAND DUSTER

Insecticide may be applied to surfaces in liquid, cream, or paste form with a paintbrush. This method often permits a more accurate placement of the material than does spraying or dusting. It is recommended where only spot treatments are needed. Cream or paste insecticides are usually available in stores where liquids and dusts are sold.

Poisoned bait, as the name implies, is a bait on which a pest will feed and to which a pesticide has been added. In the home, poisoned baits may be used to control rodents and some other pests. Frequently they are more hazardous to humans and pets than other forms of pesticide. If you use a poisoned bait, handle it with extreme care; follow the directions and observe all precautions on the container label.

COCKROACHES

Cockroaches seek warmth, moisture, and food. They hide during the day in sheltered, dark places in the home, and come out at night to forage. They feed on garbage as well as human food; because of this, they may transmit human diseases.

Cockroaches contaminate and spoil human food. They eat starch and glue, and thus may damage fabrics, garments, curtains, books, papers, and many other materials. Good housekeeping and the use of insecticide when necessary are the only certain means of keeping your home free of cockroaches.

Diazinon, malathion, or ronnel control all kinds of cockroaches. You can use a household surface spray or a dust. For a severe infestation, use both. Apply the spray first; then apply the dust after the spray has dried, forcing the dust into cracks and openings difficult to reach with a spray.

When treating cupboards and pantries, take everything from shelves and remove drawers so that food and utensils will not become contaminated by the insecticide. It is not necessary to treat the insides of drawers if you have thoroughly cleaned them. However, it is important to treat the sides, backs, and bottoms of drawers and the insides of cabinets.

HOUSEFLIES

Houseflies constitute about 98 percent of the flies that invade the home. They are among the filthiest of insect pests. They breed in decaying organic matter and feed indiscriminately on manure, garbage, and the food on our tables. They contaminate everything they touch and spread many human diseases.

Houseflies breed in places where garbage accumulates. Clean up these places. See that your garbage cans are equipped with tight-fitting lids. Promptly dispose of the droppings of pets. Do not allow food to stand where it will attract flies.

Keep houseflies out by placing screens in your windows and doors. See that screened doors swing outward. Screens that have 14 meshes to the inch will keep out houseflies; if the screens have 16 meshes, they will also keep out many smaller insects.

If you need an insecticide to control the flies in your home, apply a household or aerosol spray. Be sure the container label says the spray is for flying insects.

SILVERFISH AND FIREBRATS

Silverfish and firebrats are slender, wingless insects ⅓ to ½ inch long. They are similar in appearance. Silverfish are shiny and silver or pearly gray; firebrats are mottled gray.

These insects are active at night, and usually hide during the day. Silverfish live and develop in damp, cool places—particularly in basements. Firebrats prefer very warm areas in the home, such as the attic in summer and the furnace in winter. Both insects crawl along pipelines and through openings in the walls or floors; they may be found in any part of the house.

Silverfish and firebrats cause damage in homes by eating foods and other materials that are high in protein, sugar, or starch. They eat cereals, moist wheat flour, any paper on which there is glue or paste, the sizing in paper (including wallpaper and bookbindings, starch in clothing, and rayon).

To control silverfish and firebrats, apply insecticide in the form of a surface spray or a dust. The results may not be immediate; but if the insecticide is properly and thoroughly applied, it will leave a residue that should be effective within a few weeks. If satisfactory control is not achieved in two or three weeks, make additional applications. If you are troubled with firebrats but not with silverfish, you may need to apply insecticide only to warm parts of the house.

Use a household spray containing chlordane, lindane, ronnel, or malathion. Apply the spray to baseboards, door and window casings, closets, and places where pipes go through walls. Some sprays have oil-solution bases; do not apply these near electric motors, gas pilot flames, or other places where they may start fires.

You can also use a dust containing not more than 6 percent of chlordane, 1 percent of lindane, or 5 percent of malathion. Apply with a hand duster, blowing it into cracks and on surfaces of the places recommended for sprays. Dusts may be applied safely to places where oil-solution sprays might start fires.

MICE

At one time or another, almost every homeowner finds mice to be a source of annoyance and damage. These little rodents usually migrate from outdoor areas into homes when the weather turns cold in the fall. They eat or contaminate human food, injure fabrics, wood, and other materials, and transmit several human diseases.

The first steps in controlling mice are to seal any holes in the walls, floors, and foundation of the house and to see that food is not left in places where mice can get to it.

If there are only a few mice in your home, they can usually be disposed of with ordinary snap traps. The traps should be placed along walls and near holes. Place them at a right angle to the wall so that the trigger mechanism will intercept the mouse's probable route of travel.

One of the best baits to use in snap traps is peanut butter smeared over the trigger surface. Other good baits are cake, flour, bacon, nut meats, cheese, and soft candies, particularly milk chocolate or gumdrops.

Where mice are so numerous that trapping is impractical, poison bait may be used. Purchase materials labeled for this purpose. Follow the directions and observe all precautions on the container label.

Care should be taken to avoid placing the materials where there is danger of contaminating food supplies. Pesticides should never be left within reach of children, irresponsible persons, pets, or livestock.

RATS

Rats destroy or pollute human food, transmit diseases, and damage property. If cornered, they are dangerous and may attack people or pets. They enter homes to find food and shelter.

The first control measure for rats is to starve them. Leave no food in open places; this includes food in unopened cardboard containers. Place garbage and refuse in tightly covered metal containers.

Remove the rats' shelter. Keep storage places orderly and clean. In the basement and storerooms, stack lumber, boxes, cartons, and other objects on racks at least one foot above the floor.

Poisoned bait is recommended as the best means of killing rats. Purchase a suitable bait, labeled for the purpose. Follow directions on the label and observe the precautions to the letter. Poisons should never be left within the reach of children, irresponsible persons, pets, or livestock.

Traps are also an effective means of killing rats in the home, but their use requires skill and much time. Traps are recommended where infestations are very small, or as a follow-up after the use of bait.

Close all holes in exterior walls. See that spaces around doors, windows, and other necessary openings are no larger than ¼ inch. If rats are a serious problem in your neighborhood, install self-closing devices on frequently used doors to the outside.

Where rats are a neighborhood problem, community action should be taken; assistance should be asked of your local board of health.

PESTICIDE SAFETY

The first rule of safety in using any pesticide is to read and follow the directions and precautions on the container label. Do this each time you use a pesticide; don't depend on your memory. Many pesticide manufacturers include leaflets of instructions with their products. Carefully read these also.

Store pesticides as directed on their labels, in closed, well-labeled containers, where children or pets cannot reach them. Do not place them near food. Do not store them under the sink, in the pantry, or in the medicine cabinet.

Always leave pesticides in their original containers. Be sure the labels remain on them. If a pesticide is marked "POISON," there will be an antidote statement on the label.

Do not dispose of surplus pesticides where they may be a hazard to fish or wildlife. Do not discard them outdoors. Do not dispose of them where they may contaminate water. If you have trash-collection service, wrap small containers in several layers of newspapers, tie securely with heavy string or cord, and place them in the trash can.

Determine the right amount of the right pesticide to use.

Be careful not to get pesticide on food, dishes, or cooking utensils.

Remove aquariums, birds, cats and dogs, and other pets and their food and water pans before applying pesticide. Keep children away from application areas.

When the label warns against breathing pesticidal mists or dusts, open windows and doors first.

Wash your face and hands with soap and water after using a pesticide.

12

Simple Plumbing Repairs

E VERY HOMEOWNER is faced at some time with the aggravating "drip . . . drip . . . drip" of a leaking faucet or the endless rush of water through a toilet that won't stop running. Trying to get a plumber to come and fix these minor (but no less maddening) problems is a tedious and expensive matter—if you are lucky enough even to find one of these artisans who wants to be bothered.

The do-it-yourselfer can save much money and avoid annoying delays by making minor plumbing repairs himself. Extensive plumbing repairs or alterations in the plumbing system usually require authorization from local officials and possibly inspection of the completed work. Unless you have considerable experience, such work should be done by a qualified or licensed plumber.

REPAIRING WATER FAUCETS AND VALVES

Water faucets and globe valves serve the same purpose: they control the flow of water. The essential difference is that faucets are used at discharge points over fixtures such as sinks, lavatories, and tubs, whereas valves are used to close off portions of the plumbing system.

Other types of valves, such as check valves, gate valves, and pressure-reducing valves, are not too common in normal home plumbing. Problems with these types of valves normally necessitate their replacement.

Faucets and globe valves are very similar in construction, and repairs are also similar. (Your faucets or valves may differ somewhat in general design from the one shown, because both faucets and valves come in a wide variety of styles depending on the manufacturer. Mixing faucets, which are found on sinks, laundry trays, and bathtubs, are actually two separate

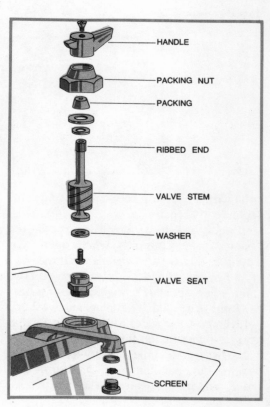

Typical faucet.

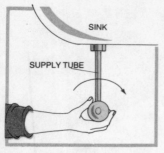

Shut off water to faucet.

Disassemble faucet.

Replace washer.

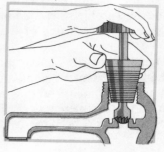

Resurface seat.

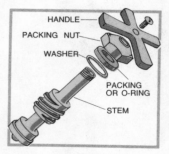

Replace O ring.

units with a common spout. Each unit is independently repaired.

If a faucet drips when closed or vibrates ("sings" or "flutters") when open, the trouble is usually a worn washer at the lower end of the spindle. If it leaks around the spine when opened, new packing or a new "O" ring is needed. To replace the washer:

1. Shut off the water at the shut-off valve nearest the particular faucet.

2. Disassemble the faucet—the handle, packing nut, packing,. and spindle, in that order. You may have to set the handle back on the spindle and use it to unscrew and remove the spindle.

3. Remove the screw and worn washer from the spindle. Scrape all the worn washer parts from the cup and install a new washer. If you do not have the proper size washer, file down a larger one; do not use one that is too small.

4. Examine the seat on the faucet body. If it is nicked or roughed, reface it. Hardware and plumbing-supply stores carry the necessary seat-dressing tool, which is sold with directions for use. Hold the tool vertically when refacing the seat.

5. Reassemble the faucet.

To replace the packing or "O" ring, simply remove the handle, packing nut, and old packing or ring and install a new packing washer. If a packing washer is not available, you can wrap stranded graphite-asbestos wicking around the spindle. Turn the packing nut down tight against the wicking.

LEAKS IN PIPES AND TANKS

Leaks in pipes usually result from corrosion or from damage to the pipe and tubing (some acid soils also corrode metal pipe and tubing). The corrosion usually occurs, in varying degrees, along the entire length of pipe rather than at some particular point. An exception would be where dissimilar metals, such as copper and steel, are joined.

Treatment (softening) of the water may solve the problem of corrosion. Otherwise, you may have to replace the piping with a type made of material that is less subject to the corrosive action of the water. It is good practice to get a chemical analysis of the water before selecting materials for a plumbing system. Your state college or university may be equipped to make an analysis; if not, you can have it done by a private laboratory.

Pipes that are split by hard freezing must be replaced. A leak at a threaded connection can often be stopped by unscrewing the fitting and applying a pipe joint compound that will seal the joint when the connection is screwed back together.

Small leaks in a pipe can often be repaired with a rubber patch and metal clamp or sleeve. This must be considered as an emergency repair job and should be followed by permanent repair.

▲Large leaks in a pipe may require cutting out the damaged section and installing a new piece of pipe. At least one union fitting will be required unless the leak is near the end of the pipe. You can make a temporary repair with plastic tubing or rubber hose. The tubing must be strong enough to withstand the normal water pressure in the pipe. It should be slipped over the opened ends of the piping and fastened with pipe clamps or several turns of wire.

Vibration sometimes breaks solder joints in copper tubing, causing leaks. If the joint is accessible, clean and resolder it. The tubing must be dry before it can be heated to soldering temperature. Leaks in places not readily accessible usually require the services of a plumber and sometimes of both a plumber and a carpenter.

Leaks in tanks are usually caused by corrosion. Sometimes, a safety valve fails to open and the pressure that is developed causes a leak. Although a leak may occur at only one place in the tank wall, the wall may also be corroded thin in other places. Therefore, any repair should be considered temporary, and the tank should be replaced as soon as possible.

A leak can be temporarily repaired with a toggle bolt, rubber gasket, and brass washer. You may have to drill or ream the hole larger to insert the toggle bolt. Draw the bolt up tight to compress the rubber gasket against the tank wall.

WATER HAMMER

Water hammer sometimes occurs when a faucet is closed. When the flow of water is suddenly stopped, its kinetic energy is expended against the walls of the piping. This

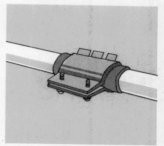

Apply pipe joint compound (above).

Repairing a small leak (above right).

Cutting away damaged section of pipe (right).

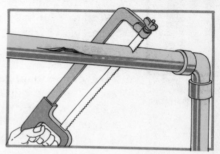

Using hose for temporary repair (left).

Resoldering a damaged joint (below left).

Temporary repair of leaking tank (below).

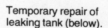
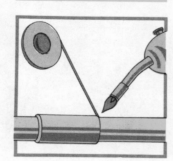
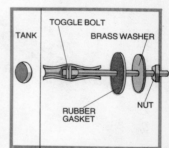

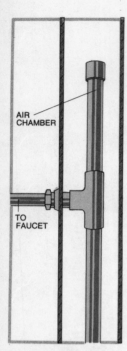

AIR
CHAMBER

TO
FAUCET

Air chamber to avoid
water hammer.

causes the piping to vibrate, and leaks or other damage may result.

Water hammer may be prevented or its severity reduced by installing an air chamber just ahead of the faucet. The air chamber may be a piece of air-filled piping or tubing, about 2 feet long, extending vertically from the pipe. It must be air-tight. Commercial devices designed to prevent water hammer are also available.

FROZEN WATER PIPES

In cold weather, water may freeze in underground pipes laid above the frostline or in pipes in unheated buildings, in open crawl spaces, or in outside walls.

When water freezes it expands. Unless a pipe can also expand, it may rupture when the water freezes. Iron pipe and steel pipe do not expand appreciably. Copper pipe stretches some, but does not resume its original dimensions when thawed; repeated freezings will cause it to fail eventually. Flexible plastic tubing may stand repeated freezings, but it is good practice to prevent it from freezing.

Pipes may be insulated to prevent freezing, but this is not a completely dependable method. Insulation does not stop the loss of heat from the pipe—it merely slows it down—and the water may freeze if it stands in the pipe long enough at below-

freezing temperature. Also, if insulation becomes wet, it loses its effectiveness.

Electric heating cable can supply the continual heat needed to prevent freezing of pipes in areas of intense cold. The cable should be wrapped around the pipe and covered with insulation.

Use of electric heating cable is the best method of thawing frozen pipe, because the entire length of pipe is thawed at one time. Thawing pipe with a blowtorch or propane torch can be dangerous. The water may get so hot at the point where the torch is applied as to generate sufficient steam under pressure to rupture the pipe. Steam from the break could severely scald you.

Thawing pipe with hot water is safer than thawing with a blowtorch. One method is to cover the pipe with rags and then pour the hot water over the rags.

When thawing pipe with a torch, hot water, or similar methods, open a faucet and start thawing at that point, thus reducing the chance of the buildup of dangerous pressure. Do not allow the steam to condense and refreeze before it reaches the faucet.

REPAIRING TOILETS

Toilets vary in general design and in the design of the flushing mechanism. But they are enough alike that general repair instruc-

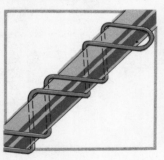

Wrap heating cable around pipe.

Thawing a pipe with hot water.

Thawing a pipe with a torch.

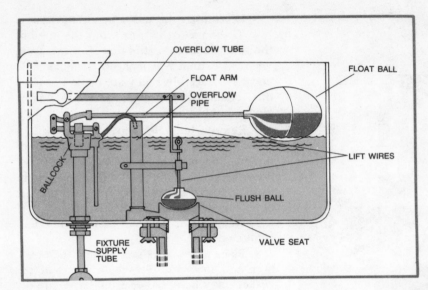

Typical toilet.

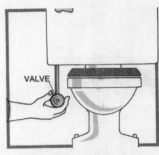

Shut off water supply to toilet.

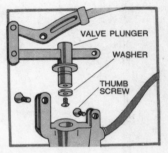

Replace washer.

tions can suffice for all designs. Parts that usually require repair are the flush valve, the intake (float) valve, and the float ball.

● The rubber ball of the flush valve may become soft or out of shape and fail to seat properly. This causes the valve to leak. Unscrew the ball and install a new one.

● The trip lever lift wire may corrode and fail to work smoothly, or the lift wire may bind in the guides. Disassemble and clean off corrosion or replace parts as necessary.

When working on the flush valve, stop the flow of water by propping up the float with a piece of wood. Be careful not to bend the float rod out of alignment.

A worn plunger washer in the intake valve will cause the valve to leak. To replace the washer:

1. Shut off the water and drain the tank.

2. Unscrew the two thumbscrews that hold the levers and push out the levers.

3. Lift out the plunger, unscrew the cup on the bottom, and insert a new washer. The washer is made of material such as rubber or leather.

4. Examine the washer seat. If nicked or roughed, it may need refacing.

If the float valve assembly is badly corroded, replace the entire assembly.

● The float ball may develop a leak and fail to rise to the proper position. (The correct water level is about 1 inch below the top of the overflow pipe, or enough to give a thorough flush.) If the ball fails to rise, the intake valve remains open and water continues to flow. A leaking float ball must be replaced. When working on the float ball, be careful to keep the rod aligned so that the ball will float freely and close the valve.

An obstruction in the toilet trap or leakage around the bottom of the toilet bowl may require removal of the bowl. Follow this procedure:

1. Shut off the water.

2. Empty the tank and bowl by flushing and sponging out the remaining water.

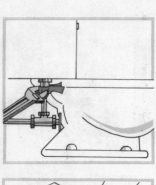

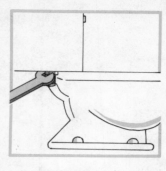

WAX GASKET

Disconnect pipe (top left).

Disconnect tank from bowl (top right).

Remove bowl (above left).

Place new wax seal (above).

Set bowl in place (left).

Level bowl (below).

3. Disconnect the water pipe to the tank.

4. Disconnect the tank from the bowl if the toilet is a two-piece unit. Set the tank where it cannot be damaged. Handle tank and bowl carefully; they are made of vitreous china or porcelain and are easily chipped or broken.

5. Remove the toilet seat.

6. Carefully pry loose the bolt covers and remove the nuts holding the bowl to the floor flange. Jar the bowl enough to break the seal at the bottom. Set the bowl upside down on something that will not chip it.

7. Remove the obstruction from the discharge opening.

8. Place a new wax seal around the bowl horn and press it into place. A wax seal (or gasket) may be obtained from hardware or plumbing-supply stores.

9. Set the bowl in place and press it down firmly. Install the nuts that hold it to the floor flange. Draw the nuts up snugly, but not too tight because the bowl may break. The bowl must be level; keep a carpenter's level on it while drawing up the bolts. If your house has settled, leaving the floor sloping, it may be necessary to use shims to make the bowl level. Next replace the bolt covers.

10. Install the tank and connect the water pipes to it. It is advisable to replace all gaskets, after cleaning mating surfaces.

11. Test for leaks by flushing a few times.

12. Install the seat and cover.

When cold water enters a toilet tank, it may chill the tank enough to cause "sweating" (condensation of atmospheric moisture on the outer surface of the tank). This can be prevented either by warming the water before it enters the tank or by insulating the tank to keep the temperature of the outer surface above the dew point temperature of the surrounding air. A tempering device that will mix a little hot water with the cold may be installed on the water-supply line to the tank to warm the water. Insulating jack-

Chapter 12 • Simple Plumbing Repairs

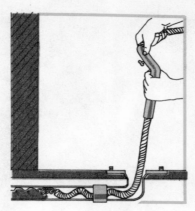

Using a clean-out auger.

Using a hose to clear clogged drain.

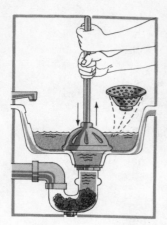

"Plumber's friend" in action.

ets or liners that fit inside toilet tanks and serve to keep the outer surface warm are available from plumbing-supply dealers.

CLEARING CLOGGED DRAINS

Drains may become clogged by objects dropped into them or by accumulations of grease, dirt, or other matter. If the obstruction is in a fixture trap, usually the trap can be removed and cleared. If the obstruction is elsewhere, other means must be used.

Cleanout augers—long, flexible steel cables commonly called snakes—may be run down drainpipes to break up obstructions or to hook onto and pull out objects. Augers are made in various lengths and diameters and are available at hardware and plumbing-supply stores. (In some cases you may have to call a plumber, who will probably have a power-driven auger.)

Small obstructions can sometimes be forced down or drawn up by use of a rubber force cup (plunger or "plumber's friend"). Water pressure from a hose may break up an obstruction or force an object on through the pipe. Wrap rags around the hose where it enters the pipe to minimize backflow of water.

Grease and soap clinging to a pipe can sometimes be removed by flushing with hot water. Chemical cleaners may also be used. When water is added, the reaction loosens the grease and soap so that they can be flushed away. Use cold water only. Chemical cleaners should not be used in pipes that are completely stopped up, because they must be brought into direct contact with the stoppage to be effective. Handle the material with extreme care and follow directions on the container. Spills on the hands or clothing should be washed with cold water immediately. If any gets into your eyes, flush with cold water and call a doctor.

Sand, dirt, or clothing lint sometimes clog floor drains (such as are found in basement and grade-level laundry rooms). Remove the strainer and ladle out as much of the sediment as possible. You may have to carefully chip away the concrete around the strainer to free it. Flush the drain with clean water. If pressure is needed, use a garden hose. Wrap cloths around the hose where it enters the drain to prevent backflow of water. You may have to stand on this plug to keep it in place when the water is turned on. Occasional flushing of floor drains may prevent clogging.

13

Simple Electrical Repairs

ELECTRICITY is probably the most conveniently applied form of energy for household uses. In addition to its great convenience and adaptability for various purposes, it has the advantage of safety when properly handled. There are, however, possible serious hazards to both life and property if electrical wiring and devices are incorrectly installed or utilized.

Electrical wiring and appliances are intended for specific functions and should be used only for the purposes for which they are intended. Electrical devices, particularly heat-producing appliances such as toasters, coffee makers, etc., should be moved only by means of the insulated handles provided. Current-carrying parts of wiring devices for appliances such as sockets should never be touched before current is cut off at the main switch.

It is important to avoid contact with electric wires or conductors in bathrooms, kitchens, laundries, basements, garages, or other rooms where floors may be damp. The danger of receiving electrical shocks is greatest under wet conditions because of the increased conductivity of the skin. Therefore, when your hands or other parts of your body are wet, do not touch electrical appliances, fixtures, or the connecting cords. Electric shock usually occurs when current flows from the live part of a device through the point of contact to a person's hands or body, with the return circuit being made either through wet feet or contact through a hand that is touching some grounded object, such as a radiator, stove, or heater. If current flow passes through or near the heart, the effects may be very serious.

Minor repairs to the electrical system and equipment of a house are the only ones that should be undertaken by an inexperienced home handyman. These include such tasks as replacing a blown-out fuse, replacing broken or frayed appliance cords, or overhauling a doorbell system. Unless you have considerable electrical experience, do not attempt to disturb or extend permanent wiring. Work of this nature should be done by a licensed electrician in accordance with local regulations or the provisions of the latest edition of the National Electrical Code.

DISCONNECTING ELECTRICAL CURRENT

The entire supply of electrical current may be cut off where it enters the house system by pulling or disconnecting the main switch, which is usually located in a metal box in the basement.

Each adult member of the household should be familiar with the means for disconnecting the current. The method of operation varies according to the type of design. In some equipment, a handle protrudes from the box or enclosure, and the circuit is disconnected by pulling the operating lever down; on circuit breakers or pull-out type switches, the method of opening is on the outside of the box.

FUSES AND CIRCUIT BREAKERS

The wires in each house circuit are intended to carry a certain load current and if overloaded they may become heated and cause a fire. Fuses or circuit breakers are used as safety devices to guard against this danger. When more than the rated current load is placed on the circuit wiring, the safety device operates, opening the circuit. This is called "blowing" a fuse or "tripping" a circuit breaker. Before service is restored, the cause of the blown fuse or tripped circuit breaker should first be determined. To do this, the appliance that was put on the line at the time the fuse blew should be disconnected. If the fuses on this particular branch again blow, an electrician should be called in and no further effort made to use this circuit until the trouble has been located and corrected.

If an electrical circuit is overloaded by connecting too many appliances to it at one time, a fuse may blow or a circuit breaker trip. A short circuit, which may also blow a fuse or trip a circuit breaker, may be caused by faulty electrical insulation.

Since fuses are intended to protect the wiring of a circuit, it is important when replacing them to use those of the proper rating. Branch circuits in residences are usual-

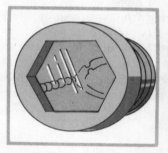
Fuse.

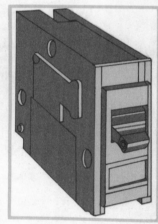
Circuit breaker.

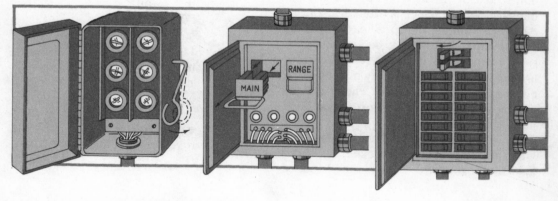
Main switch types.

ly wired with No. 14 or No. 12 wire and are intended to be protected with fuses rated 15 or 20 amperes, respectively. The 20-ampere circuits are used in kitchen, breakfast-room, and laundry-appliance circuits. The 15-ampere fuse or circuit breaker protects the usual lighting circuits. Appliances that draw heavy currents should not be connected to lighting circuits because their wires are not designed to carry heavy loads. Electric ranges and water heaters are usually installed on separate higher-voltage circuits where the rating of the fuses corresponds to the rating of the devices. Only approved fuses should be used.

Before replacing a fuse, open the switch controlling the circuit affected or the main switch, to avoid possible shock. Fuses should be replaced by those of the same rating, as fuses of higher capacity will not protect the wiring from overheating, thus defeating the safety purpose for which they were intended. The main switch need not be disconnected when resetting a circuit breaker; flip the switch. If cartridge fuses blow, call the utility company; the problem may be major.

APPLIANCE CORDS AND PLUGS

Wear and damage to appliance cords and plugs are common occurrences in the home, usually as the result of abuse rather than age. An appliance is often disconnected with a yank on the cord instead of a tug on the plug. Wires may be routed under rugs where there is much foot traffic, or around hot radiators. Or they may be casually stapled to woodwork. These are the most common causes of short circuits and nasty shocks.

You should inspect appliance cords regularly for signs of frayed, cracked, or broken insulation, and check plugs for damaged prongs and loose terminal connections. When any of these conditions exist, the cord or plug must be replaced.

It is important that the replacement match the appliance to which it is being fitted. Lamps, radios, televisions, and other low-power devices can use standard light-weight cord and any standard rubber or plastic replacement plug. Heavy-duty braided or rubber cord should be used for vacuum cleaners, power tools, outdoor extension lamps, and large appliances. Toasters, irons, hot plates, and any heating appliance should have special heat-resistant cord—any other type will invite trouble.

The most common type of plug has terminal screws to which the cord wires are attached. Yanking a cord to remove the plug from the outlet usually results in the fraying or cracking of the insulation just behind the plug or its terminal connections coming loose. If the plug and cord look intact otherwise, and prongs and insulation are in good condition, simply disconnect the cord at the terminals and pull it through the plug until you reach insulation that is intact.

Cut the cord at this point, then separate the two wires to a length of about 1½ inches. With a sharp knife, strip ½ inch of insulation from each end, taking care not to cut through the wire. Twist the wire ends so there are no loose strands. Loop each wire

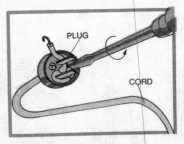

Disconnect cord from terminals.

Strip off insulation.

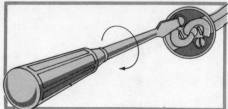

Twist strands of wire (far left).

Wrap around terminals (left).

around a prong and wrap the wire around the terminal screws in the same direction the screw will be tightened.

Some plugs are sealed and have the cord wires connected directly to the prongs. In this case you must cut off the plug and install a new one.

For heavy-duty plugs and cords with braided or heavy rubber insulation, cut about 3 inches off the cord's outer insulating material but leave the inside insulation for the individual wires intact. Then tie the two ends into an "Underwriters' knot," which will fit snugly into the base of the plug. This is designed to prevent wires from pulling loose from the terminals when subjected to sudden tugs, as they would be with any heavy-duty appliance that has to be moved around. Once the knot has been made and tested for fit, strip ½ inch of insulation from the wire ends and connect as described above. It is a good idea to use the Underwriters' knot on any appliance that has a plug large enough to accommodate the knot.

With light-duty cord, simple snap-on plugs may be used. These are fitted firmly over the end of the unstripped cord; movable prongs pierce the insulation to make contact with the wire, as well as to provide a firm grip.

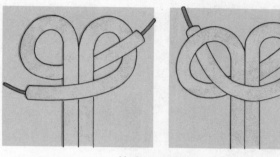

Underwriters' knot.

Snap-on plug.

LAMP REPAIRS

When a lamp fails to light and the trouble is not with the bulb or a short in the wall circuit, the cause is either the plug, the lamp

wire, or the socket. First check the plug for good contact. If it fits loosely in the wall outlet, try bending the prongs apart a bit. If the lamp does not light, check for loose wires at the plug terminals. If the plug prongs are loose or if the plug looks in any way doubtful, replace the plug, as described previously.

Sockets don't often need replacement, but if they incorporate a switching device the switch may wear with use, and the entire socket must be replaced. Unplug the lamp and remove the bulb. The socket assembly is in two major parts, a cap fixed to the lamp base and a brass shell that snaps

Press to snap off shell.

Disconnect wires.

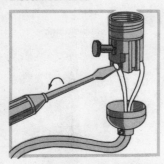

PRESS

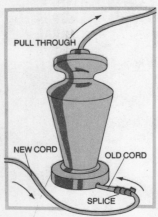

PULL THROUGH

NEW CORD

OLD CORD

SPLICE

Using old cord to bring new cord through lamp.

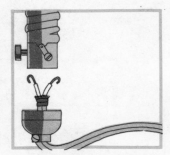

Replace switch assembly.

into that. Inside are a combined switch and socket plus a cardboard or fiber liner that protects against short circuits. Snap off the shell by pressing at the point indicated at the base of the shell, then remove it and the liner to gain access to the switch. Disconnect the wires and remove the switch. The cap can be left in place and the other parts replaced as an assembly, available in any hardware outlet.

It is often difficult, if not downright impossible, to thread a new cord into a lamp by probing, particularly on tall floor units. A simple solution is to cut or disconnect the plug of the old wire and attach one end of the new wire to that. Make the temporary splice as secure and slim as possible. Dis-

connect the old cord at the lamp socket and pull gently until the new cord emerges through the fixed socket cap. Connect to the socket or switch and replace the shell. Then attach a new plug.

DOORBELLS AND CHIMES

When a bell or chime refuses to sound, the first thing you should check is the push-button. Remove the button cover and inspect for loose connections. If all are tight, either bridge the button terminals with a piece of wire or paper clip or disconnect the wires and touch the bare ends together. (The voltage across the terminals is minimal, so do not worry about shocks.)

If the bell sounds, the trouble is in the button and it should be replaced. If it does not sound, you should check the power supply, a transformer usually wired alongside or near the main fuse box. The output terminals of the transformer can be bridged with a screwdriver. (Never touch input terminals—these are wired to the house

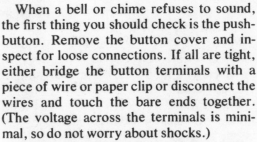

Check button contacts.

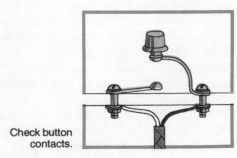

TRANSFORMER

TO POWER SOURCE

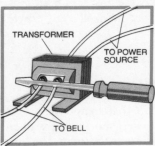

TO BELL

Check transformer.

110-120 volt current and can give a severe shock.) If sparks appear, power is coming through and you should look elsewhere.

If voltage is not coming through the transformer, either the fuse to the circuit is blown or the transformer has burned out.

If there is power, the next thing you should check is the chime or bell. Remove the cover or housing and look for dirty or sticking parts and broken connections. Sand contact points if they appear pitted or corroded. With chimes, check for free operation of the small rods that move to strike the chime bars. Clean as required.

When bell or chimes, pushbuttons, and power supply check out and all visible connections are tight, the trouble is in the wiring. Repair in this case is best left to the electrician.

Sand contact points on bell.

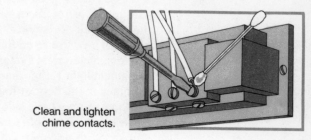

Clean and tighten chime contacts.

14

Storm Damage

Homes and furnishings damaged by flooding, windstorm, or tornado need prompt clean-up action. Before entering a damaged building, be sure that it is not about to collapse. Turn off gas at the meter or tank and let the house air for several minutes to remove foul odors or escaped gas. Do not smoke or use open flame until you are sure that it is safe to do so. Do not turn on an electrical system; it may have become short-circuited. After dark, use a flashlight rather than a lantern to avoid igniting escaped gas. Watch out for holes in the floor or loose boards with exposed nails.

Flooding may have swollen doors tight. When entrance must be forced because of swollen doors, accumulated mud, or bulged floors, enter by a window or other opening. Lift the pins from door hinges with a screwdriver and hammer. Be sure the door is unlocked and then carefully push it in from the outside to avoid further damage.

Loose, wet ceiling plaster is heavy and dangerous. Knock down hanging plaster before moving around in the house, and watch for loose plaster as the structure dries out.

Use even greater caution if damage resulted solely from high winds. Tornadoes may demolish some buildings and move others almost intact some distance from their foundations. Before entering or cleaning a tornado-damaged building be sure that walls, ceiling, and roof are in place and that the structure rests firmly on the foundation. Look out for broken glass and broken power lines.

Remove the window sash.

Remove the molding holding the window.

DRYING AND CLEANING

Open doors and windows to admit air that is essential to dry the house. To open swollen windows, remove the small strip that holds the lower sash. Carefully use a chisel to avoid marring woodwork. Force the sash up slightly and remove from frame by pushing it from the outside into the hands of a helper. Be careful not to break the glass.

Examine foundations and basement walls for signs of undermining. If settling or cracking has occurred, it may be necessary to dig down to the footings and reinforce or replace settled sections. Undermined footings should be reinforced with masonry or concrete, never with earth or gravel. Tilted or settled piers may need replacing. If the building is out of plumb or the floors have settled or bulged, make sure that the foundation is sound and that sills, girders, and joists are free from termite damage before renovating. If the building must be moved, call in expert help unless the structure is a simple one.

Drain and clean basements as soon as the building is safe. Pump or bail the water from the cellar and shovel out the mud while it is moist so that basement floors can dry. Remove mud from the furnace, flues, and smoke pipe.

Don't rush to move in. The house must be clean and dry before it is habitable. Drain pools of water from the premises; remove and burn or bury driftwood, rubbish, and decaying vegetation. If the house or porches rest on open foundations, be sure the structure will not collapse before removing debris from underneath.

CHECKING THE ELECTRICAL SYSTEM

Do not turn on lights or appliances until an electrician has checked the electrical system for short circuits. Wear rubber-soled shoes or boots and rubber gloves. Turn off the main switch while standing on a dry board. Use a piece of rubber, plastic, or dry wood when touching the metal handle of the switch box. Water in conduits or connection boxes and dampness on exposed wires can cause short circuits and fires. Under these conditions, a person replacing fuses may even be electrocuted, especially if standing on a wet surface.

If a sump pump is available and needed, remove all fuses except the main fuses and the one controlling the sump pump. Carefully turn on the main switch to see if the pump operates. If not, call an electrician.

ELECTRIC MOTORS

Small electric motors may be dried in an oven at not more than 150 degrees F. If you are accustomed to working with electric motors, test them after six or eight hours of drying. If there is still evidence of grounding or short-circuiting, return them to the oven for two to four hours before testing again. If you are not accustomed to working with electric motors, do not risk electric shock; have the motors tested by a technical expert.

MECHANICAL HOUSEHOLD EQUIPMENT

A competent technician should examine pump motors, refrigerators, freezers, ranges, washing machines, vacuum cleaners, food mixers, and other household equipment. They may be ruined if they are not clean, dry, and free-running before the current is turned on.

Washing machines should be thoroughly cleaned before use. Open the gear housings and clean the shafts and gears with kerosene. Wipe all parts with a clean cloth, but do not force any dirt into the bearings. Even fine grit can cause wear of moving parts. Wipe metal surfaces with a rag dampened with kerosene to remove rust and dirt stains. Coat them thinly with petrolatum or machine oil to prevent further rusting. Before using, oil the bearings and, using a soft cloth, dry surfaces exposed to hands or clothing.

The cooling systems and motors of modern refrigerators are hermetically sealed. Their construction should rule out damage

Remove mud from chimney flue.

Repair chimney mortar.

by immersion in water. In older refrigerators, the cooling unit is accessible and should be cleaned and examined.

For safety, technicians should inspect household machines and make repairs, especially of motors and power-driven appliances. It may be practical to arrange cooperative employment of electricians to collect and recondition motors in a shop.

CHECKING THE HEATING SYSTEM

Before starting a fire in a hot-air heating plant, examine the inside of the heater and wash sediment from the flues with a hose or a swab on a long stick. Often, flues can be reached through a clean-out door above the fire door. Or you may have to remove the smoke pipe and do the cleaning from that end. If the heater is jacketed, clean out all mud between the inside and outside casings, removing the outer casing if necessary. If flues or passages are choked with mud, a boiler may burst when a fire is started. Take the smoke pipe out of the chimney and reach through the thimble to remove mud from the lower part of the chimney flue so that there will be a draft for the fire. An inadequate draft may fill the house with smoke or dangerous carbon monoxide.

In oil-burning systems, have the storage tank examined by an experienced inspector to make sure that seams have not opened, permitting dirt or water to enter. The burner should be dismantled and all parts cleaned in kerosene and wiped dry. The air blower and fuel pump should be examined. Gear housings should be removed and the gears thoroughly cleaned with kerosene. Any remaining grit will cause undue wear. Make sure you burn kerosene-soaked rags out-of-doors. Do not wash them in an automatic washer; this may cause an explosion.

Chimneys subjected to wind or water action should be inspected promptly. Defective chimneys can cause fires and carbon monoxide gas poisoning. Disintegrated mortar in the joints between bricks should be replaced with masonry cement. If the chimney has settled badly or broken where it passes through floors or roof, it may need rebuilding. If the chimney has tilted, see if the footing has been undermined.

WATER SUPPLY AND SANITARY SYSTEMS

If your water comes from a well, cistern, or spring, ask your local health department to check it for safety and to tell you how to keep it safe. If water from a surface source must be used, take the supply from a point upstream from any inhabited area, dipping from below the surface. Avoid sources with odors, dark color, or floating material.

In an emergency, limited amounts of water may be obtained by draining a hot water tank or by melting ice cubes.

There are two general methods for disinfecting small quantities of water: boiling and chemical treatment. Boiling is the most positive way to make water bacterially safe. Certain chemicals, if applied with care, will free most waters of harmful or pathogenic organisms.

The effectiveness of the disinfectant method is reduced in turbid or discolored water. First, filter such water through clean cloths or allow it to settle; draw off the clear water to be disinfected and store it in clean, tightly covered, noncorrodible containers.

A 10-minute boiling will kill any disease-causing bacteria present. The flat taste of boiled water can be improved by pouring it back and forth from one container to another, by allowing it to stand for a few hours, or by adding a small pinch of salt for each quart of water boiled.

When boiling is not practical, chlorine or iodine are commonly added to the water for disinfecting. A chlorine solution may be prepared from one of three products:

1. Common household bleach, by following the instructions on the label, or by finding the percentage of available chlorine on the label and using this table:

Available Chlorine* (percent)	Drops per quart of clear water**
1	10
4–6	2
7–10	1

*If strength is unknown, add 10 drops per quart to purify.

**Double amount for turbid or colored water.

Mix the treated water thoroughly and allow it to stand for 30 minutes. If the water does not have a slight chlorine odor, repeat the dosage and allow it to stand for an additional 15 minutes. The treated water may be made more palatable by allowing it to stand for several hours or by pouring it between two clean containers.

2. Granular calcium hypochlorite, in a ratio of 1 heaping teaspoon (¼ ounce) to 2 gallons of water, makes a chlorine solution that will disinfect water. Add 1 part of the solution to 100 parts of water or, roughly, 1 pint to each 12.5 gallons.

3. Chlorine tablets in commercially prepared form may be obtained from drugstores or sporting-goods stores. If there are no instructions on the package, use one tablet to each quart of water.

Either tincture of iodine or iodine tablets may be used to purify water. Add five drops of 2 percent United States Pharmacopeia (USP) tincture of iodine to each quart of clear water. For turbid water, add 10 drops and allow the solution to stand for at least 30 minutes.

Use commercially prepared iodine tablets according to directions or add one tablet for each quart of water. All water used for beverages, cooking, or brushing the teeth should be properly disinfected.

Test plumbing and basement drains by pouring in a bucket of water. If the water does not run out, remove the clean-out plug from the trap (a U-, P-, or S-shaped pipe found under most fixtures) and rake out mud and debris with a wire. Toilet and drain traps can be cleaned with water and a swab, or by rodding with a plumber's "snake" or a wire.

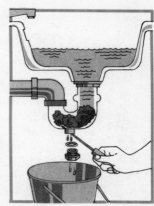

Remove clean-out plug, clean trap.

Clean toilet trap with auger.

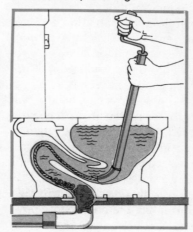

▲ It may be necessary to disassemble and clean check valves and other backflow preventers. In wind-damaged houses all exposed pipes should be checked for intact connections before water is turned on.

Swamped sanitary disposal installations imperil health. The domestic water supply is almost sure to become contaminated. Septic tanks, cesspools, pits, and leaching systems must be put in service at once. Local or state health departments or the United States Public Health Service can provide useful advice on cleaning, repairing, or relocating installations.

Local or state health departments have responsibility for enforcing health measures and a trained staff to help you. Problems relating to water purity, waste disposal, or rodent control should be referred to them. Also, they can help with many insect problems that are often storm-related.

Some garbage can be burned. Garbage that will not burn should be buried in a pit 4 or 5 feet deep and covered with at least 18 inches of soil. Garbage fed to pets or other animals should be cooked to prevent spread of disease.

ODORS

Basement odors, although unpleasant, are usually harmless. If ventilation does not remove them, sprinkle bleaching powder (chlorine of lime) on the floor, allow it to remain until the floor dries, and sweep it up. This powder is a good disinfectant.

But bleaching powder is caustic and poisonous. Before sprinkling it on the basement floor, read the label on the container. Follow instructions and heed precautions. Keep bleaching powder out of children's reach and away from eyes and mouth. Provide ventilation with doors and windows open while sprinkling the floor. Store powder in a closed container away from mois-

ture. Dispose of empty containers in a tightly covered refuse can.

Dry lump charcoal exposed in open containers may absorb odors from the air in enclosed spaces. But charcoal is highly combustible when moist or wet, so guard against spontaneous combustion and fire. Expose it in tin cans or other hard metal, open containers away from flammable liquids and gases, cloth, coal, firewood, or other readily combustible materials. Store charcoal in a well-ventilated place where it will be dry and clean.

FLOORS, WOODWORK, DOORS, WALLS

After the wet mud has been removed, floors may be badly buckled. Do not attempt repairs until they are fully dry. Start the heating plant as soon as it will operate, but don't use so much heat that the house becomes steamy. Dry wood as fast as you can without aggravating shrinkage or deformation. Open windows and doors wide for good ventilation, but maintain a temperature of at least 50 to 60 degrees F.

When the house is dry, some of the buckled flooring may be drawn back into place with nails. Some humps may be removed by planing or sanding. Heavily planed floors may never look well uncovered, but a smooth old floor can serve as a base for new flooring. If smooth, an old floor may be covered with a resilient, smooth surface floor covering. If the damage is too severe, new flooring may be necessary. If only the surface finish is damaged, the floor may be refinished.

Before the house is dried out, scrub woodwork with a stiff brush, plenty of water, and a detergent to remove mud and silt from corners and cracks.

Quickly drain accumulated water from partitions and exterior walls so that insula-

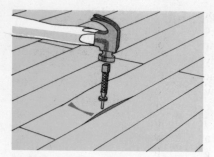

Nail down buckled floorboards.

Remove baseboard, drill holes for drainage.

Mildewed floors, woodwork, and other wooden areas may be scrubbed with a mild alkali, such as washing soda or trisodium phosphate (4 to 6 tablespoons to a gallon of water). Paint stores and grocery stores sell these products under various trade names. Rinse well with clear water and allow the wood to dry thoroughly. Then apply a mildew-resistant paint. Mildew-resistant paint contains fungicide and should not be used on playpens, cribs, or toys.

If mold has grown into the wood under paint or varnish, scrub with an abrasive cleaner, then wash with a solution containing 4 to 6 tablespoons of trisodium phosphate and 1 cup of household chlorine bleach to a gallon of water. Finally, rinse the wood well with clear water. Dry thoroughly and apply a wood preservative before repainting.

Locks should be taken apart, wiped with kerosene, and oiled. If you cannot remove them, squirt in a little machine oil through the bolt opening or the keyhole, and work the knobs to distribute the oil. Otherwise, the springs and metal casing will soon rust and need replacing. Do not use so much oil that it drips onto the woodwork and makes later painting difficult. Cleaning and oiling usually puts hinges in order.

tion and structural members can dry. Remove the baseboards and drill holes between the studs a few inches above the floor. After the insulation and frames have dried, replace the baseboards.

For a final, thorough washing of floors, use your preferred cleaning product—nonsudsing is best. Put off necessary refinishing until moisture has dried from the framing, from between walls and floors, and from the back of the trim, even though this may take months. Consult an experienced painter about refinishing. If you do the work yourself, carefully follow instructions on cans of standard brands of paints and varnishes for household use.

Use heat and ventilation to thoroughly dry mildewed wood. Badly infected wood may need to be replaced, preferably with wood that has been treated against mildew or that is naturally decay-resistant.

Squirt oil in and work lock.

Clean and oil hinges.

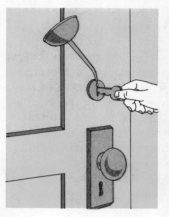

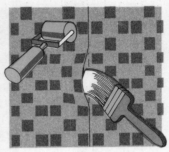

Repaste loose wallpaper edges.

Wash walls from bottom up.

Allow the plaster to dry thoroughly before washing it. Brush off any loose surface dirt. Wash painted walls with water and mild soap or any commercial cleanser. (Professional renovators usually prefer nonsudsing products.) Use two sponges and two buckets, one for the cleaning solution and another for clear rinsing water. Start washing the wall at the bottom and work up, so that water will not run down and streak a soiled area. Water running down over a clean area can be wiped off without damage. Wash an area that you can easily reach without changing position; rinse it immediately. Then wash the next area, overlapping the first, and proceed until the wall is finished. Ceilings should be done last. Badly stained walls will need redecorating.

After walls have been cleaned and before wallpaper is replaced, paint or thoroughly spray the walls with a quaternary disinfectant, available from janitor- or dairy-supply outlets. Add 2 tablespoons of disinfectant to 2 gallons of water. This prevents mildew and may be applied on both painted walls and washable wallpapers.

Often, wallpaper is so discolored and brittle from soaking that it must be removed and the walls repapered. If the paper remained dry but has been loosened by dampness, it may be possible to repaste loosened edges or sections. Use commercial wallpaper paste.

Clean wallpaper with a commercial puttylike cleaner. Some wallpapers are washable. Before washing, test a small inconspicuous spot using mild soap or detergent. Proceed as for washing a painted wall. Squeeze as much water as possible out of the cleaning and rinsing sponges and work quickly so that paper does not become soaked.

Grease spots may be removed from wallpaper with a paste made of dry-cleaning fluid with cornstarch or talcum. Allow to dry and brush off, repeating if necessary. Fumes from all dry-cleaning solvents are toxic and some are flammable. Use only with adequate ventilation, and read the precautions on the label.

SALVAGING FURNITURE

Move wooden furniture outdoors and take out as many drawers, slides, or other working parts as possible. Do not force

Remove back of furniture to push out drawers.

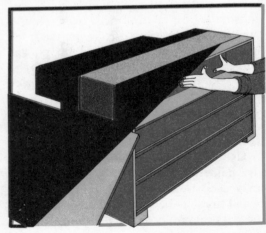

stuck drawers with a screwdriver or chisel from the front. Remove the back, by cutting out if necessary, and push out the drawers. Clean away all mud and dirt, using a hose stream if necessary. Take the furniture indoors and store it where it will dry slowly. Do not leave furniture in the sun, as it will warp and twist out of shape.

▲ Some furniture, especially that made of solid wood, may be salvaged by regluing. Gluing usually requires the use of a variety of clamps. First, decide if you wish to invest in this equipment and have the time and skill to do the work. If not, consult a cabinetmaker.

▮ Repairing veneered furniture is difficult and requires so many different types of tools that it is not practical to try at home. A cabinetmaker should do this job. Otherwise, the furniture may be returned to the factory for repair by the store where it was purchased. If insurance allows part value on flood-damaged furniture, it may be financially wise to apply the allowance on new articles rather than to pay for repairs to damaged items.

Furniture that has not been submerged may have developed white spots or a whitish film or cloudiness from dampness. If the whole surface is affected, try rubbing with a cloth and turpentine or camphorated oil; wipe dry at once and polish with wax or furniture polish. If color is not restored, dip 3/0 steel wool in oil (boiled, linseed, olive, mineral, lemon) and rub lightly with the grain of the wood. Wipe with a soft cloth and rewax. For deep spots, use a drop or two of ammonia on a damp cloth. Rub at once with a dry cloth, then polish. Cigarette ashes rubbed in with the fingertips are often effective in removing white spots. If all efforts to remove white blemishes fail, refinishing may be necessary.

Brush outer coverings of upholstered articles, mattresses, rugs, and carpets to remove loose mold. Do this outdoors to avoid scattering mildew spores in the house. Run a vacuum cleaner attachment over the surface. Dry the article with an electric heater, a fan, or any convenient method. Sun and air the article to prevent mold growth.

If mildew remains, sponge upholstery or mattresses lightly with thick suds of soap or detergent; wipe with a clean, damp cloth. Use little water on the fabric to avoid soaking the padding.

Another method for upholstered furniture requires wiping with a cloth wrung out of diluted alcohol (1 cup denatured alcohol to 1 cup water). Dry the article thoroughly.

With a low-pressure spray containing a fungicide, moisten mildewed surfaces thoroughly. Aerosol spraying is not effective in controlling fungi.

Be careful not to inhale mist from a spray or use near flame. Follow all precautions on the label.

In closed areas, vapors of paradichlorobenzene or paraformaldehyde will stop mold growth. If molds have grown into the article, it should be dried and fumigated by a dry-cleaning or storage company. Fumigation will kill existing mold but will not protect the article in the future.

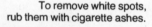

To remove white spots, rub them with cigarette ashes.

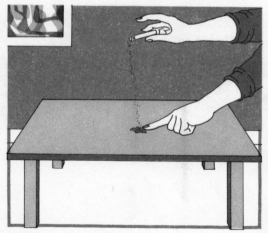

Badly damaged upholstered furniture that has been submerged may need re-stuffing. Springs may need to be cleaned and oiled, and the frame may need cleaning. If you are not skilled in this work, consult a cabinetmaker or upholsterer.

Clean metal at once, especially iron. Wipe rust from iron with a kerosene-soaked cloth. Coat iron hardware lightly with petrolatum or machine oil to prevent further rusting. Use stove polish on iron-work. Wash cooking utensils thoroughly with soapy water to remove kerosene, then rub with unsalted cooking oil and heat slowly to permit oil to soak the pores of the metal for rust-resistance.

Stainless steel, nickel-copper alloy, or metals plated with nickel or chromium need only thorough washing and polishing with a fine-powdered cleanser. If the plating is broken, exposing the base metal to rust, wipe with kerosene, wash and dry the surface, then wax for rust-resistance.

Wash aluminum thoroughly and scour unpolished surfaces with soap-filled metal scouring pads. Polished or plated surfaces of aluminum should be wiped with silver polish or fine cleaning powder.

To brighten darkened insides of aluminum pans, fill with water and add ¼ cup of vinegar or 1 tablespoon of cream of tartar for each quart of water. Boil for 10 to 15 minutes, then scour with a soap-filled pad. If utensils have been submerged in flood water and are darkened both inside and out, prepare one of these acid solutions in a large container and immerse them; then proceed with the treatment described.

Copper and brass can be polished with a special polish or with salt sprinkled on a piece of lemon or on a cloth saturated with vinegar. Wash utensils after treatment.

15

Emergency!

Nᴏᴛ ᴇᴠᴇʀʏ ʜᴏᴜsᴇʜᴏʟᴅ emergency poses a hazard to life, limb, and property, but when the house is plunged into darkness or the toilet bowl is overflowing and water is cascading down the stairs, it seems serious enough—and it is. You should always plan for the worst, and then hope that your planning is for naught. But if you should be called upon to administer "first aid" to a household malady, either while waiting for a repairman to wend his way to your home or as a stopgap until you can make permanent repairs yourself, it is best to "Be Prepared."

One of the basic preparations is to have an emergency toolbox ready to be whisked to the scene of the problem. For the tools you should have on hand, see ᴄʜᴀᴘᴛᴇʀ 4. In addition, you should have a good flashlight—preferably several of them placed in strategic spots throughout the house. It's a good idea to check periodically to make sure that they are still where they are supposed to be, and that the children have not borrowed them for a backyard camping trip or to play midnight tag. Check also to make sure that they (the flashlights) are in working order. When an emergency does occur, dead batteries are an aggravation you really don't need.

Like a well-run ship, the well-run home should be ready to deal with emergencies. All family members should be acquainted with certain procedures and fixtures, such as shut-off valves and circuit breakers. When (if) something does go wrong, you can't expect to head for the family library and look for this book to tell you what to do. This is one chapter you should study in advance and be ready to put into practice as soon as it's needed. Quick action in an emergency can prevent costly damage to materials, furnishings, and equipment—and, in some situations, to the family members themselves.

● PLUMBING EMERGENCIES

Here are the most common emergencies that may occur and the action to take. The name, address, and phone number of a plumber who offers 24-hour service should be posted in a conspicuous place near your telephone.

Burst pipe or tank—Immediately cut off

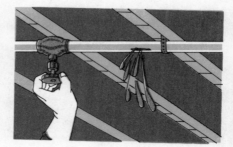

Close shutoff valve nearest leak.

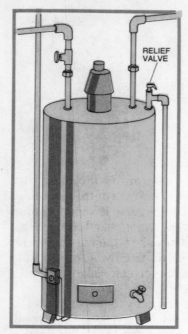

RELIEF VALVE

Check pressure relief valve to find out whether it is operative.

Closeup of pressure relief valve.

Shutting down the plumbing system:
1. Turn off electricity or gas to heating units.
2. Close main valve.
3. Open faucets, flush toilets on top floor.
4. Open faucets, flush toilets on lower floors.
5. Open drain valves on heaters, etc.
6. Pour antifreeze into toilets, drains.

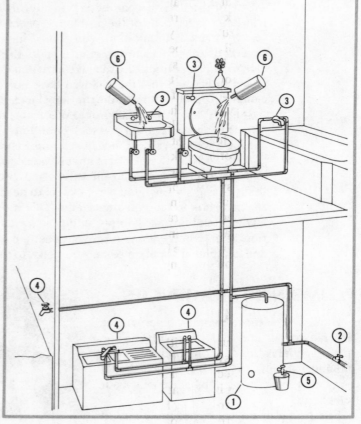

the flow of water by closing the shutoff valve nearest to the break. Then arrange for repair.

Toilet overflow—Do not use toilet until it is back in working order. Check for and remove stoppage in bowl outlet, or in drain line from closet to sewer or septic tank. If stoppage is due to root entry into pipe, repair of pipe at that point is recommended.

Rumbling noise in hot-water tank—This is probably a sign of overheating, which could lead to the development of explosive pressure. (Another indication of overheating is hot water backing up in the cold-water supply pipe.) Cut off the burner immediately. Be sure that the pressure-relief valve is operative. Then check (with a thermometer) the temperature of the water at the nearest outlet. If above that for which the gauge is set, check the thermostat that controls the burner cutoff. If you cannot correct the trouble, call a plumber.

Cold house—If the heating system fails (or if you close the house and turn off the heat) when there is a chance of sub-freezing weather, completely drain the plumbing system. A drain valve is usually provided for this purpose at the low point of the supply piping. A pump, storage tank, hot-water tank, toilet tank, water-treatment apparatus, and other water-system appliances or accessories should also be drained. Put antifreeze in all fixture and drain traps.

Hot-water and steam heating systems should also be drained when the house temperature may drop below freezing.

FURNACE FAILURE

When you find yourself without heat, first check the main switch. It may have been accidentally turned off (not an uncommon occurrence when it is located along a basement stairway where it may be brushed against by a person carrying a load of laun-

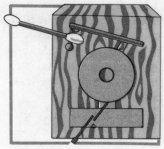
Check thermostat for dust.

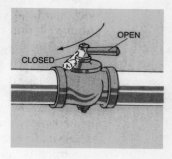
Check gas valve.

dry or whatever into the basement). Also check for a blown fuse or tripped circuit breaker.

Take a look at the thermostat to see whether it has been turned down. Often, the obvious will be the cause of the problem. Remove the thermostat cover and inspect the workings for dirt or dust that may be clogging the mechanism.

Next check the fuel supply. If you have oil heat, look at the gauge atop the storage tank. If it is near the "Empty" mark, you can suspect that this is the cause of your chilly discomfort. Call for a refill. With gas heat, make sure that an intake valve has not inadvertently been shut off.

GAS ODOR

When you detect the odor of gas, get everybody out of the house—fast! Don't tarry, but if there is time, turn the furnace thermostat all the way down so that the burner doesn't come on, possibly setting off an explosion. Needless to say, don't strike a match or light up a smoke to calm your nerves. Keep everyone at a distance and call the local gas company immediately, preferably from a neighbor's phone. If this is not possible, and the gas odor is not too strong, hold a handkerchief over your nose and reenter the house to call the utility—or just dial the operator and explain your problem. Then get back outside, and don't go into the house again until the servicemen have come and repaired the leak. Above all, don't take chances!

FIRE

Fire is the dread nightmare of most homeowners and apartment dwellers, and it deserves to be. But prompt and proper action upon the discovery of a household fire can minimize the danger, at least to the inhabitants. Unfortunately, all too often a homeowner will attempt to battle a "small" blaze himself, only to lose precious minutes and have it develop into a total holocaust.

Train all members of your family to shout "Fire!" as loudly as possible at the first sign of flames or smell of smoke. They should, of course, be warned against deliberate false alarms (crying "Wolf!"), but an accidental false alarm is better than no alarm at all. Everyone in the house should be aroused and flee. Never linger to save possessions—they are not worth a life!

Next (not before) call the fire department. As mentioned above, it is best to do this from a neighbor's house. In most cases, you need simply dial the operator. Be sure to clearly state your full address.

If the fire is confined to a small area and you have a safe and sure exit available, you can reenter the house and use an extinguisher or water to fight the blaze until the firemen arrive. But be certain you know what you are doing. Don't, to use an obvious example, throw water on a grease fire—it will only spread the flames. If there is any question of your own safety, do not try to fight the fire yourself. Homes are replaceable (and usually insured). People may be insured, but they are not replaceable.

Once again, the key to avoiding disaster is prevention. Make sure that every member of the family knows what to do in case of fire. Every room should have an alternate escape route; rooms on upper floors should have windows that are easily opened. If there are not lower roofs onto which occupants can jump, provide rope ladders or similar means of descent, and make sure that children are well acquainted with their use.

You will probably never have to put these precautions into practice. But if you do, lives will be saved.

Rope ladder for upper stories is helpful.

Index